The

P.R.I.M.E.

P artnering
R esources
I n
M inistry
E ducation

FACTOR

A Radical
Philosophy
of
Collaborative
Education

John H. Morgan

THE P.R.I.M.E. FACTOR
(Partnering Resources In Ministry Education)
A Radical Philosophy of Collaborative Education

by John H. Morgan

ISBN 1-929569-12-2

Printed in the United States of America

Published on behalf of the
Graduate Theological Foundation
www.gtfeducation.org

by

The Cloverdale Corporation
Cloverdale Books
South Bend, Indiana
cloverdaleusa@aol.com

To Robley Edward Whitson,
who encouraged me
to think outside the box.

TABLE OF CONTENTS

INTRODUCTION

Beyond Cookie-Cutter Professionalism:
Pursuing a Better Way!

This book is about innovative post-credentialed professional education generally but specifically in the human services field of ministry and its cognates – pastoral work, education, health care, administration, counseling, and mediation. The focus will be upon the development of a creative mechanism whereby leading educational programs can be clustered such that both the professional student can benefit as well as the institutional programs themselves. The interest here is not in creating yet another educational program, venue, conference, or workshop, but rather the development of a packaging mechanism whereby the professional student can take advantage of the best programs available and where the providing institutions can likewise benefit. The students, in other words, will benefit from the clustering of excellent options of study and the providing institutions can benefit by attracting students to their programs.

As it now stands, post-credentialed professionals desiring to further their education must select one institution from which to take the desired degree and the prescribed courses from the institution's own in-house faculty. What the P.R.I.M.E. Factor proposes to do is to provide these same students an opportunity to select from a variety of attractive educational venues with just those courses suited to their particular and well-thought-out needs and package those into a degree program. This procedure thereby enhances the range of educational component selections while maximizing the tailoring of a carefully and individually crafted degree program.

This process to be explored in this book, called the P.R.I.M.E. Factor (Partnering Resources In Ministry Education), consists of these components, viz.,

(1)   assessment and evaluation of the student's professional and academic training upon
entry into a terminal degree program,

(2)   the crafting of a well-designed personalized educational goal as dictated by the student's background, present situation, and professional ambitions,

(3)   selection of just those educational venues which address the student's carefully developed professional study plan, and

(4)   the management and monitoring of this study plan to its completion.

Through assessment, educational goal development, study plan, and management, the student moves beyond the faculty and curriculum restrictions necessarily imposed by a single institutional framework to a world of educational opportunities packaged into a carefully developed tailor-made degree program which addresses personal needs rather than institutional requirements.

Chapter One

The Problem

Institutional Limits, Faculty Fatigue, Student Aspirations

From the outset I wish to emphasize the category of student being addressed in this book. The interest here is not the undergraduate student just coming into the university fresh from high school. Heaven knows, they need all of the institutional structure and support available, as we will all agree, for university life is fundamentally a postponement of maturity and the prolongation of adolescence with a little learning thrown into the cauldron for good measure. Only the naïve suppose that university life is all about learning with a little social life thrown in for good measure. If one were able to compress the actual learning which occurs during a four year collegiate residency, we would not be surprised to find it taking no longer than three or four months of actual learning! Indeed, the postponement of maturity and the prolongation of adolescence is the primary agenda of the university, and it has consistently done a good job of it. In fact, the job has been done so well that now when employers bring on a fresh college graduate, they find that the new recruit has to be trained from ground zero in most cases in order to fill the bill. The concept of the experienced rookie went out with the old-fashioned apprenticeships of bygone days, and more's the pity too, if you ask me.

Also, and we must keep this point in mind throughout this discussion of a radical philosophy of collaborative education, we are not speaking here of the first degree graduate student, those who have gone directly from the undergraduate curriculum to pursue an advanced degree. Many times, this movement from undergraduate to graduate study has become a pro forma agenda for the more mature student and, therefore, upon finally leaving the halls of learning, they are sufficiently trained and equipped to take on gainful employment that the time spent earning the graduate degree, usually only one or two years (and in the case of the clergy and lawyers, three years), is thereby justified.

Rather, that constituency which will be addressed in this book has to do with the seasoned post-credentialed advance-degreed professional: that individual who early on took both the undergraduate and graduate degrees and commenced a professional career. But now, twenty or so years into the professional practice of some form of ministry – parish life, administration, counseling, mediation, teaching, etc. – they find themselves desiring and/or in need of a topping off of their training in order to reach either their own personal expectations or those of the institution within which they find themselves working. These professionals – seasoned veterans with graduate degrees and several years of experience under their belts – are the ones to be addressed herein. If we forget the specific constituency being addressed in this book, much of what will be said will sound foolish and irresponsible.

Let it be said from the outset that there is a place, a rightful and needful place for colleges and universities, with their faculties, libraries, campuses, sports programs, social life for maturing youngsters, and a lively alumni and faithful parents paying tuition to keep them going. Without them, where would the high school graduates go except into the workforce of the country, often well

4

before they have sufficient maturity to do so responsibly? Yes, the social learning and skill development which occur in colleges and universities today are important for future success. And the prolongation of adolescence and the postponement of maturity have their rightful and needful place in American society. But for our purposes here, we will hold up the seasoned veteran professional as the focus of our discussion and the development of what we believe to be a viable and needful alternative paradigm of professional education alongside the traditional cookie-cutter institutionalized curriculum promoted by the academic community today.

The Institution

We have what we have and that's all that we have!

There are basic components in higher education needed by all colleges and universities, more or less, in order for them both to do their work and to convince the public that they are doing it. These institutional needs include a facility, a campus, a library, a faculty, and an administration for the development and enforcement of rules and regulations. Certainly for the undergraduate, and even the first graduate degree institutions, these things are indispensable, but only more or less. The fact that a facility must be situated on a sprawling campus of trees and walkways may be disputed, but the image itself constitutes the demand for such. A president of a major Midwestern university once told me that the keeping of the building and grounds of his institution was one of the most important "symbols" of learning, to say nothing of one of the most expensive components of the institution's operating budget, for which the university had to assure continued enrollment and on-going alumni support. So the "symbolic" value alone of the buildings and campus is sufficient to justify their existence.

Now, one might argue that if the college or university would locate between a city park and the public library, the need to maintain a campus and the need to fund a library would be greatly diminished. The simple act of bringing together the publicly tax-supported city park and the publicly tax-supported city library would so reduce the operating costs of a college that pressures to continue fundraising might be somewhat reduced and, more importantly, the prospects of reducing the tuition charged to students and parents for the privilege of "going to college" as well. If the maintaining of buildings and grounds coupled with the establishment and continued maintenance of a library constitutes two major expenses of a college, why not remove those costs by carefully selecting the location?

We have bricks, books, rules, and regulations.

Now, for the students "going off to college," these things, these symbols if not their realities, are important both to assure students that they are really "going off to college" and that the tuition being paid by themselves or their parents is really justified. How much of the college selection process is determined by the "beautiful campus" has never been measured, but my forty years of experience on the campuses of some of the greatest universities in America and England have convinced me that the "campus beauty" is extremely important in the selection process. Otherwise, what do parents and students see when they arrive "on campus?" Yes, and at the end of the day (or the four years!), the correlation between the beautiful campus and the education gotten for the money is difficult to measure if not to identify.

The same might be said of the library. Walking the aisles of a multi-storied library might have its symbolic value but to what extent the thousands of books on the shelves have actually directly impacted and benefited the average student on campus is up for serious inquiry and discussion. It is possible to get through even some of our greatest universities without spending more than a token moment or two during the freshman year in the library! Indeed, studies have shown that a good percentage of graduating seniors from college have spent only the slightest amount of time in the library "actually using the library." Much of the clock time

6

spent in the library by undergraduate students has to do with using the facility as a study hall or a social arena for party planning. The relationship between physical presence of the student in the library and the actual purposeful and effective utilization of the library holdings is tenuous at best and increasingly suspicious given the access to "real research opportunities" on the internet.

As for the seasoned veteran professional, the whole question of "campus life" becomes a moot point. For them, it's not about bricks and mortar at all; it's all about the learning! For professionals who have "done the college scene" during their earlier maturing years, the campus life is irrelevant. Furthermore, for these veterans, the learning experience is existentially applicable, not theoretical. The interest and intent in pursuing the terminal degree for the experienced professional is career related, immediately linkable to a rung on the ladder, an advancement within the workplace, rather than the collegiate agenda of "getting a job." For these individuals, the bricks and mortar are no longer a "symbol of learning," but, at most, the evidence needed by the institution to justify exorbitant tuition costs for the learning being pursued and the education being offered.

The buildings and grounds must be kept.

Of course, the "fabric" of the learning space must be maintained; indeed, in most instances it must be downright attractive, otherwise, students won't come and parents won't pay. The relationship, however, between nicely cut grass and the learning of physics is somewhat tenuous, though symbolically essential for the justification of fees for the promised education. Now granted, there is no institutional commitment to the graduating student that what they have learned will get them a job, indeed, that is a subject that is taboo in many hallowed halls of learning. Nevertheless, there is the inevitable "promise of success" which comes from earning a degree from a college with a beautiful campus. It might be the unusual undergraduate who perceptively sits in the classroom wondering what building his tuition is paying for, but rest assured, such musings more often than not characterize the minds of the veteran professionals who have

7

"done their duty" by taking the undergraduate degree but now seek really to gain from the learning experience and not just pay for more grounds-keeping maintenance.

The books and the library must be used.

If the veteran professional is somewhat jaded about the relationship between tuition and the brick edifices on campus, such feelings of resentment or skeptical disillusionment are more quickly aroused when one turns one's thoughts to the college library. As an expensive study hall where quiet is maintained as the cultural environment and where study carols become scenes of caballing party-planning ne'er-do-wells, the library for the undergraduate serves its purpose. But, as the locus of learning, the seat of scholarship, the nexus of insight, one might dare suggest that the college library is none of these as a general rule. More often than not, it's the college dorm or the graduate student's flat or the nearest off-campus coffee shop or pub or internet café in which the lofty learning experiences are found to be flourishing. Why should a seasoned veteran professional be subjected to the problematics of "getting themselves off to the library" when what they need to advance their careers by taking the terminal degree is as close as the nearest internet server? Why the fuss about going to the library, paying library fees, "checking out books" assigned by the faculty? Why not access what is needed over the internet, at one's own convenience, in one's own learning space where ever that may be? My institution, which does not maintain a physical library nor a physical campus (we use the internet and are adjacent to a city park!), provides the incoming doctoral-level student with a forty-page directory of internet libraries, most with full texts either free or nearly so. Just one website, Pub Med, provides the American Medical Association library in full-text for ten cents a page for all published medical journals in English for the past fifty years! Beat that in your local research library, and there is no cost to the degree-granting institution and students can use the library anytime, anywhere, and virtually at no cost. More on this point later.

8

The rules and regulations must be followed.

One of the systemic problems with colleges and universities offering multiple levels of training – bachelor's, master's, doctorates – is that, for the most part, the faculty and the administration are the same personnel for all three levels. Granted, there are some institutions which exercise the luxury (or is it a rip-off to students?) of maintaining a graduate faculty but still and all there is a redundancy of faculty and staff in the multi-levels of degree program development and execution. Therefore, when once the process of developing a set of rules and regulations is put in place, curriculum development, degree programs, etc., there is the inevitability of repetition of formula. So we have rules and regulations governing the bachelor's degree with its appended curriculum (albeit with "flexibility" built into the electives offered to students) and, likewise, we have rules and regulations governing the master's and the doctorates with their appended curricula as well. Thus, there is the similarity of degree programs at all three levels. Might there be room for a level of student-directed selectivity at the doctoral level, especially for seasoned veterans returning from years in the field?

The professionals of whom I speak are those quite suited to know what they need prior to commencing their studies. Indeed, they often are the most informed in the fields of study to which they are attached. Whereas the jaded faculty of tenured acclaim may not have been "in the field" for years, even decades, these professionals are fresh in from the trenches. Shouldn't they be given the right and responsibility of setting the curriculum, designing the rules, implementing the degree requirements? Certainly the faculty, more often than not, would stand to learn a great deal in this interactive process. Faculty at the War College in Washington, DC, regularly bring in seasoned officers from the fields of battle to teach them what is now happening. Medical Colleges and Law Schools consistently do the same. Why should any doctoral-level seat of learning presume that the wisdom is embodied in the faculty when the incoming student is a seasoned veteran professional right out of the muck and fray of battle?

The Faculty

They are ours, so use them!

Issues aside regarding the institutional framework and fabric of books, buildings, rules, and regulations, another major component of consideration and controversy these days centers around the faculty itself. Not that faculty aren't needed, or wanted, or appreciated; rather, who and why and when and where and how are there to be faculty constitute the concerns. In our present consideration, we are not speaking of undergraduate education but rather advanced post-credentialing graduate, and particularly doctoral-level, education. In the Europe of old, there were "independent" professors in various fields of learning who hung around the university offering tutorial assistance to the struggling and to the ambitious students in need of a boost. They were called "privatdozents." Much of that tradition has been lost in the U.S. and, alas, in Europe as well and, we believe, to the disadvantage and distress of all concerned.

We hire the best we can and hope they improve.

The problem and problematics of securing and maintaining a high-level graduate faculty for doctoral-level training of already credentialed professionals become obvious when one takes into account the speed with which professions are advancing in knowledge, skill, and applicability. To secure a highly qualified faculty in any field is not particularly difficult given the number of Ph.D.'s academic institutions are churning out, often with little or no regard for the destiny of those graduates. However, to "maintain" this same faculty at a consistently high level of performance is an altogether different matter. Once tenure is obtained, it is, alas, rather easy to rely increasingly upon one's old notes, the same old tired texts, the same old dated and decrepit stories for the general amusement of a captive, albeit not unappreciative, audience of graduate-level professional students.

10

They have degrees and write books.

Now, of course, we all know what is expected of faculty at universities. They teach courses (the lower down the food chain the more courses they teach such that at some Ivy League schools the green room definition of a full professor is one who is perpetually on leave!). They read papers at distinguished and preferably international conferences which results in travel and adventure. And, they should, if worth their tenured salt, write the occasional odd book, the more esoteric and specialized the better. The hiring of faculty at such a level at such institutions of learning as are being discussed here is itself an adventure. For, contrary to the paying parents of undergraduate tuition, these faculty are not expected to be either trained in or gifted at the actual "teaching" part of the title "Professor," but rather more skilled at those functions which accrue merit and benefit to the institution granting tenure, viz., reading papers and writing books.

The notion that a "Professor" is actually gifted at "professing" is too often far from the mark. I was once told at a major university where I had just been hired that if I intended to get on well there and reach tenure, I had better make the students hate me as quickly as possible for, if not, I would never get any "real work" done, by which was meant papers written and books read. For, as the argument goes, the students, seeking encouragement and assistance in the learning process, would never leave me alone. The faces of the jaded old men and women on the tenured line-up of the department testified to the virtue of the admonition. Like the young beginning medical students who have to have the love of the patient and the love of the treatment pounded out of them so they can really get on with the business of learning to practice medicine and accrue wealth for themselves which is expected of their colleagues, young academic faculty must quickly learn that "teaching" and "working with students" is the dead end road of their profession which leads to termination or, even worse, being banished to the faculty ranks of the junior or community college! Oh no, even the technical college!

"Of the making of books, there is no end" says Solomon of Scripture. Of the writing of books, there seems to be no end either. I have held appointments at more than one institution which placed in their faculty contracts the requirement that the faculty person produce a major book in the field within the first three years of the appointment or the contract would be terminal. On the other hand, I have colleagues at Oxford University who have been teaching for years who have not only never written a book but have not even considered doing so. There, it seems, the actual "teaching" of students is the priority and a book, when it comes, is a natural and inevitable "overflowing" rather than the *raison d' etre.*

So what if they are not on the cutting edge anymore?

Recently, a newly appointed president of one of the Big Ten Universities in the country was overheard saying that within ten years he hoped that thirty percent of his faculty would be "contract faculty" rather than "tenured faculty." The explanation was simple and to the point (and, if I might add, to the jugular vein of the eavesdropping faculty present), namely, that for most of the curricula categories at the university, the best and the brightest in those fields were working in the private sector at the cutting edge of the subject matter rather than standing in the classroom, a talking head, reciting the same old drivel which filled the lecture notebook from the same old, occasionally "revised," textbooks. Why do the same old faculty persons teach the courses in biochemistry which they have been teaching for thirty years when an institution can hire a young, fresh, on-the-cutting-edge professional with a brand new Ph.D. working in a chemical research lab in the city and, for a tenth of the cost, give the university student the best of the best? A fair question?!

If you don't take our courses, what happens to the tuition?

Yet and to be fair, the university must ask the question, "If students don't take our courses, how are we going to get the tuition needed to maintain the buildings, books, and faculty?" Well, we are not dealing specifically with the undergraduate college which, as we all know too painfully, has its own plethora of problems and issues these days (such as dealing with legitimate concerns of students paying large sums of money for an education which seems consistently insufficient to secure gainful employment outside the ranks of the haggard Wal-Mart part timers!). Rather, we are attempting to address professional and graduate education at its highest ranges of access and viability. Thus, the asking of the question about tuition and courses seems not out of place here. And, not to put too fine a point on it, how institutions of merit justify to themselves, the public, and the consumer, the exorbitantly high costs of their educational offerings?

When one considers that some leading universities, I dare not mention their names here but they are readily known to those who need to know, charge upwards of $500 and $600 and even $700 per credit hour for a course which is also being offered at another institution, less worthy for not having had the privilege of being cited in *Newsweek* or the *U.S. News and World Report*, which charges $100 or $75 and even in one case known personally to be in Detroit of $50 per credit hour, one wonders about equity. Then, when one looks at the credentials of the actual faculty persons teaching the courses, there is absolutely no direct correlation between cost and educational training of the faculty. I know of faculty with the highest credentials in their field from the leading institutions in the world teaching at institutions with the lowest possible tuition. Furthermore, and what is more to the point, many of the best trained people in their various fields are not tenured faculty members at academic institutions at all but rather find themselves happily, or not, in other venues of service, running institutes, workshops, conferences, publishing, the private as well as the public sectors of civil and entrepreneurial service.

So in a world where one might imagine seasoned professionals seeking the best of the best in terms of faculty, they may readily discover that it is, on occasion, outside the hallowed halls of the university where the best can be found. Then, of course and inevitably, the question arises, how can I take advantage of the learning situation with such a person when the university requires me to use its books, its buildings, and its faculty? How can I gather my learning experience from the best while not conforming to the cookie-cutter mentality of a traditionalist environment which says, you must use our books, our faculty, follow our rules, if you are to secure the advanced degree? Why can't the process be consumer-driven rather than institution-driven?

The Student

Why be caught between bricks, books, rules and faculty burnout?

Now, of course, we are coming to the core of the problem, namely, that the advanced and seasoned professional student, as a matter of fact, knows better than the institution what is needed and wanted for the advancement of their own careers. It becomes an institutional bother when such seasoned students begin to assert their own independence, insinuating their own insights into their future and their careers. Unlike the physicians of old who diagnosed the problem and prescribed the medication with no questions asked, institutions today can no longer get away with that sort of paternalistic domination of experienced professionals who more often than not know more about what is occurring in the profession out in the world than the tired and jaded faculty who have been hiding in the sheltered environment of a tenured post within the university.

But I'm middle-aged and a professional, by the way!

Yet, to let the student speak is to open up Pandora's Box, for if one asks their opinions and solicits their insights, you might just get them, and then what? The physician who begins to explain the diagnosis and the medication prescribed may find himself or herself in a learning situation from a patient who is better read on the subject than is the practitioner. In the old school, better never let the student begin to ask questions at all, but rather take notes, take exams, read books, follow rules, and finish the course and then on the way with them. No questions, no problems.

What we are talking about here is addressing the reality of the professional world of experience and training in which mid-career credentialed individuals find themselves working. We are not here addressing the eighteen year olds who come to the university for a four-year hiatus from their maturity and shelter from a demanding world. Right and proper it might be for institutions to exercise a high hand in supervision and surveillance in such cases. But when it comes to credentialed professionals, why do institutions assume the same rules and procedures applying to the high school graduate which must likewise apply to them as well – use only our books, our faculty, follow our rules, take our curriculum, comply with our circumscribed degree programs. Might it be that the seasoned professional has even a better idea about what should be studied and what is needed than the resident faculty?

I have spent forty years watching and studying higher education. My latest book on the subject is entitled, *UNFINISHED BUSINESS: The All-But-Dissertation Phenomenon in American Higher Education (A National Study of Uncompleted Doctoral Degrees in Theology)*. I will have more to say about this point later on, but for now let me just say that the systemic flaws within the educational process itself should be and can be addressed. However, it will take committed institutional leaders as well as academic faculty to do so, and to date, neither seems to be willing. Of particular interest to me have been seminary education and the institution itself, the history of which is fascinating and under explored. One amazing characteristic is the high frequency of faculty teaching pastoral studies who themselves have never served a parish! Or, even worse, those who have served a parish thirty years ago and are still, even now in the classroom, using the models of ministry which seemed to have worked then.

15

Failure on the part of educational institutions to recognize, acknowledge, and, indeed, take advantage of the experience of seasoned professionals returning to them for advanced study is a real travesty and tragedy in today's cookie-cutter world of educational formula and programs. Instead of drawing from the experience and insights of the incoming veteran, the institution protects itself from their potentially intrusive contributions to the overall educational process by using preset rules and regulations for degree completion. Why not embrace their experience, nurture their insights, solicit their contributions?

The Big Ten president mentioned earlier was right, it seems, to be suspicious of the ongoing development of tenured faculty, and well he should be, as both faculties and educational administrations too often seem to be more committed to securing their own positions than to fostering the development and advancement of the incoming seasoned professional seeking an opportunity to grow. It is fair to say that to many faculty and administrators, such veteran professionals are intimidating in the learning environment for they, not the faculty, are more often than not the ones who are on the cutting edge of the profession and, thus, become the teachers of the teachers.

What building am I painting with my tuition?

To further exacerbate this conflicting matrix of a would-be learning environment, the question can rightly be asked, "Who should be paying who for this learning experience?" How many times have I overhead faculty saying, either amongst themselves or to their students, that they had learned as much or more from the encounter with these veteran student professionals than the students had. If such is the case, who should be paying the exorbitant tuitions? Or, more to the point, might there be another way to imagine a proper "educational venue" for these veteran professionals seeking yet higher levels of training? If the graduate school is not the proper place owing to its overall commitment to maintaining deteriorating buildings and shoring up its fatigued faculty, then why not envision another paradigm of learning, a

16

paradigm which recognizes, acknowledges, and affirms the experience "brought to" the learning environment by these veterans in the field? "Boot Camp," to use an unfortunate military metaphor, is certainly not the place for the seasoned warrior in from the fields; but there surely must be a place for the veteran to gain insight, grow in vision, feel nurtured in learning.

For institutions to "stay the course" by using the undergraduate paradigm of educational formulas, rules, and regulations by simply applying them to the graduate student and veteran in the field may be easier for the faculty and administration but is far from what is being asked for and what is so clearly needed by the veteran professionals. To continue to pile on the tuition charges for the old un-workable and un-working paradigmatic model of cookie-cutter education is insufferable. That the tuition is needed to paint the buildings, to cut the grass, to buy yet another hardcopy of a book which is already online in full text, goes without question. Yet, why should veteran professionals have to pay for it when they bring to the campus more than what they find there upon arrival? When houseguests bring their own food and linens, can one rightly charge B & B rates? Rather, in many instances, the host should pay the guest.

I know of countless, yes, countless, instances where the arriving veteran professional, called a "graduate student" in the institution's glossary of time-bound terms, comes into the learning environment of the institution already more qualified to teach the curriculum than the resident faculty. Just one instance will do for illustration. I know of a major Midwestern Catholic university which required of an incoming doctoral student three years of residency and $120,000.00 in tuition for the Ph.D. when that student had been on a Catholic seminary faculty in Ireland for fifteen years, recognized as the authority in his field and published to the gills, but, alas, did not have the required M.A. degree as defined by the university to be advanced to the two-year residency requirements. And, to add insult to injury, one of the graduate courses being taught at that university was using the book written by the incoming student! From "rules for rules' sake," saints

17

preserve us.

Do I need the library when I'm on the internet?

Another striking dynamic in this muddle of students caught between bricks and books, rules and faculty, has to do with the meaning, nature, and definition of "the library." Canon John Macquarrie, a colleague of mine at Oxford and the retired Lady Margaret Professor of Divinity of Christ Church College in the University, once observed to me that "in the old days," the definition of a scholar was linked to the skill and ability to go to the library and retrieve the desired texts. "Scholarship as library retrieval skills," he called it. Today, a twelve year old can find whatever is desired by way of texts over the internet – "Googling one's way to an education" as the saying goes. In my institution, we provide the incoming veteran professional not with a physical library to which he or she must regularly show up and use but rather a forty page directory of full-text libraries in every cognate field of graduate studies. We have students all over the world doing doctoral level research within the comfort of their own homes using the very same materials one would use if resident on the campus of a leading institution.

How can one define "library holdings" in a world where, and at a time when, the "World Wide Web" is our reality? The origin of the usable book, one might say, can be plotted back to Gutenberg (and the unnamed Chinese inventor) and his movable type. With that development, first published were Sacred Scriptures, of course, and then, century by century, the proving of Solomon's pronouncement, "Of the making of books, there is no end." Today, some 50,000 new titles are published in this country annually; add three times that for the rest of the world, so that it might be fairly said that we have published plenty. Of books, however, we do not have nor ever will have enough. Books are written for a purpose, to fill a need, to address a problem, to contribute to the accumulation of knowledge, enjoyment, rancor, evil, goodness, etc. And, we have libraries, old and new, dating from the late Middle Ages, books printed by presses and designed

18

to be user- friendly, albeit they may weigh twenty pounds and be chained to a post in the village square, yet, still and all, to be used. In this country (let us not dally about the history of libraries elsewhere in the world, as fascinating as that is and about which hundreds of books have been written), we owe a debt of gratitude to Benjamin Franklin for the development of what eventually became the public library. It was, in the first instance, a private subscription library designed for book readers in the villages of early America to have a place to share their few books amongst many friends.

Now, with the coming of academic institutions, the first such library we would presume was John Harvard's little stash of 200 divinity tomes set aside for the founding of Harvard College. Since then, Harvard has managed to scrape together another two million volumes, albeit not just in divinity. Early, then, there was the notion, now we wonder if it was an ill advised and ill conceived notion, that the "public" library bought and paid for by the town would be separate and apart from the "college" library which was bought and paid for by the students of the town!

It seems not to have bothered the founding fathers of our country that a duplication and, thus, a redundancy, were built into the whole notion of a "public" and a "college" library in the towns of New England. And, of course, both have suffered because, namely, the town has suffered from a diminishment of utilization by the students of the town and the college has suffered because of the unnecessary duplication of resources. Imagine a mid-size town like I live in with 200,000 people, one main library, four branch libraries, and five colleges and universities. A local librarian suggested to me recently that probably 75% of the titles are duplicated five times within a ten mile radius of each other. That a college and a public library might imagine pooling resources and providing one even bigger and better library seems not to have occurred to anyone.

Then, we complicate the matter of duplication with the internet libraries of which there are thousands, some bibliographic, but many full texts, and not just books but magazines and scholarly periodicals as well. And, with the U.S. government's projected goal of having the Library of Congress online in full text within twenty years, imagine both the unnecessary duplication of books in the country and the waste in tuition fees buying books which are never taken down from the shelves. Don't get me wrong, I love books. I have a few thousand of my own, a habit of often buying instead of reading, but, nevertheless, a fine library.

I'm reading the same books as the faculty!

The question is not, "Do we need libraries?", rather, what kind and where do we need them? For five colleges, three of which are strictly commuter colleges, within ten miles of each other to have five libraries with texts of which 75% are duplications seems both a waste of money and a folly of planning and collaboration. If one must have a physical library in order to be a college, one might want to rethink what the purpose of a college is in the first place, for it is surely not simply to provide a place for students to get and read books. If that were the case, a public library sitting beside a Borders Book Store might be just as effective and much less expensive. And, when we deal with veteran professionals returning with their hard-earned advanced credentials, more often than not they already have the major texts in their chosen fields of expertise and so end up reading the same books as the faculty they are paying to teach them. Furthermore, and more to the point, the internet provides a quick and ready access to one-time-use texts and published materials without the expense and encumbrances of a physical library!

Chapter Two

The Old Solutions

Attempts at Reviving the Last Dinosaur!

The problems posed to an academic institution by these seasoned veteran professionals seeking terminal credentialing are multiple in number and layered as well. Maintaining a campus and facilities for the undergraduate constitutes the primary and overarching responsibility for virtually all institutions of higher learning in this country, with the exception of a few very distinguished and forward-looking seats of learning such as the Institute for Advanced Studies at Princeton and Rockefeller University in New York, institutions that only offer doctoral or post-doctoral education.

For most higher education institutions, the formula for dealing with students runs about the same whether they are eighteen years old from a high school in Iowa or in their mid-fifties and a CEO of a major corporation, viz., line up the courses, have the student take them in sequence, write an exit project, and graduate. Never mind that the course line up was done by a fatigued, jaded and out of touch faculty who themselves have not been real practitioners of what they teach for years, if ever. Never mind the inconvenience to such veteran professionals as to require a one, two, or three year "residency" period on campus to secure the degree (arguing that "being close" to both books and faculty is indispensable for the learning process!). The "process" looks ever so similar from one degree to the next, whether undergraduate or graduate, just more of the same, piled higher and deeper.

I am reminded of the time our oldest child was defined by the school system as "gifted," and, therefore, the system had in place a mechanism for dealing with just such precocity. It seems they had received a grant from a very perceptive and insightful state and federal government! When we inquired as to the way this advanced child would be dealt with in terms of the curriculum and classroom performance expectations, the simple answer seemed to be they just gave them more work. In other words, the only difference between a regular student and an advanced one is the quantity of work given. Too often at the collegiate level this is the only distinguishing (indistinguishing) mark between an undergraduate and a graduate degree, never mind the terminal degree requirements and never mind the difference between a fresh eighteen year old just off the farm and that of a twenty-five year trench warrior from within the professional ranks.

"Moving the courses around might help!" muses the institution.

So the collegiate institution must become "creative" in its pursuit of the customer. "Recruitment" at institutions of higher learning is almost a unique phenomenon in American higher education. The notion that colleges and universities must spend a substantial portion of their budgets to find a sufficient number of students to pay the tuition needed to keep the doors open so they can continue to recruit students to continue to keep the doors open is an amusing story told to European and Asian academics. Rather than screening applicants who come to them, most are eagerly searching for student customers to wine and dine and tease into enrolling. Even the top institutions, in their own way, are never not marketing themselves.

And, when it comes to postgraduate or post-credentialed education at the terminal level for seasoned professionals, the hunt for customer students becomes intense. I have been told by senior administrators at such institutions many times that this "recruitment" enterprise constitutes the single largest part of the operating budget. When one asks where does all of the tuition go, one learns the same old college problem of maintaining a library, a campus, a refectory, a seated (or standing) faculty, etc.

Let's find the students and make them pay our tuition.

Student recruitment, whether for the eighteen year old or the twenty-year veteran, is a tricky business. It poses the old Groucho Marx dilemma of having students apply to a program that one wouldn't wish to belong to if it accepts someone like one's self. In other words, the need to look exclusive while plying one's wares on the street corner is immense. If exclusivity is measured by the number of times the provider says "no" (as in book publishing), then an academic institution has a problem, for every "no" means a possible decline in revenue, and without revenue, the grass doesn't get cut and new books don't get bought – never mind that the city park has its grass cut by the tax-paying public and the books for the city library get bought by the same tax-paying public. Finding the customer student then becomes the passion and, given the fact that academic institutions are normally not sterling in their market savvy (save for the University of Phoenix, maybe), much of the passion goes ungratified. Or, as too often happens, colleges with business departments offering courses in marketing, go outside and hire a marketing firm to do the dirty deed themselves. Is this ironic or have I missed something?

I was on the faculty of a distinguished university several years ago when the decision was made by the administration to hand over the management and operation of the campus bookstore to a large national franchise. When I asked why its operation was not taken on by the business department and used as a training laboratory for business majors, the reply from the dean's office was, "We never thought of it." A similar occurrence took place at a nearby college that offered a specialization in the culinary arts when the college invited a national fast food franchise onto the campus to run the college refectory. When institutions fail to draw from their own faculty resources to run their operation, one begins to questions those institutions' confidence in the instruction they offer to the paying customer student.

Is Wal-Mart a good place to host a lecture?

Creativity is called for in finding that elusive student of which every other academic institution is in search. Thus, imagination, creativity, innovation (skills not immediately associated with collegiate institutions) are called for if the problem of revenue maintenance is to be responsibly addressed. Colleges as well as advanced institutions of higher learning have experimented with a variety of alternative venues for the offering of their wares, no matter that a bit of "inter-institutional collaboration" might have gone a long way to solve the problem of serving students wherever they are. No, every institution is a new creation and each newly created wheel must address the same problems as if they were their very own.

To ask the question, "Why not collaborate with other similar institutions in sharing the responsibility for maintaining a faculty, curricula, etc?," seems not to come up. Rather, we ourselves must address every problem with the resources that we have, no matter that 2,500 other similar institutions are addressing the same problems in the same manner with the same resources. So one ends up with a stripmall approach to higher and professional education. Go to them, compare their wares, and make your choice. So why not offer one's courses at Wal-Mart? I see that Subway has moved in, they have optometrists now, churches are renting space on Sundays, and the growing presence of daycare centers means that more and more people are passing through the aisles of Wal-Mart throughout the day and night, every day of the year. When apartment complexes are being built adjacent to or attached to the Wal-Mart micro-world, why not just teach the curriculum in a booth along the wall of the Wal-Mart world of reality?

There is something to be said for taking the institution to the consumer instead of expecting the consumer to come to the institution any longer. Once freed of the notion of the "must have" library, refectory, the faculty, the bookstore, and the campus, institutions might just be freed up to concentrate on what they should be doing best, viz., education. The library can be bought and maintained by the city and so can the campus. The bookstore can be maintained by Borders or Barnes & Noble or the Wal-Mart Book Department. The refectory need no longer be a drain on the college budget; just locate next to a Taco Bell or McDonalds or Subway. Forget the campus expense when the city maintains the parks with tax money at no expense to the college. Just provide the student with a map of the town with the city parks marked plainly and be done with it. The only thing Wal-Mart can't do (yet!) that colleges and professional institutions can do is offer top-level educational opportunities. And, if a college were really smart, they would contract with Wal-Mart to use the facility as a business-training laboratory for their own students.

I can't seem to compete with the CD-Roms out there.

And then there is the burgeoning of educational software which seems to be advancing on the tried and true (if not stayed and recalcitrant) curriculum devised by the tenured faculty of bygone days. If one goes to Circuit City or Best Buy and wanders up and down the aisles of software products, it becomes obvious rather quickly that a great deal of usable education can be gotten for the price of a CD – self-help and instructional CD-Roms covering every conceivable subject, practical and impractical – physics, higher math, how to build a good rabbit cage, how to fish, auto maintenance, accounting (at all levels all the way up to Enron!), etc. And these weren't thrown together by some rabble of disenchanted youth in their parents' garage, but, more often than not, the leading scholars at the best institutions have brought to the microchip the best of the best for instructional purposes. Now, granted, many are, at the moment, built around the false pedagogical notion that the "talking head" is the only way to go so you put in the CD and find yourself staring directly into the face of a talking educator. But, that will change in time, and soon, we expect. Given the scope and sophistication of the current software, we expect any day now to see instructional CDs that are actually visually engaging.

The problem and the challenge, then, to academic institutions is to prove to the skeptical and wary public that what they have to offer on their campus with their tenured faculty is better than what can be bought for the price of a CD at Circuit City. This is a hard sell when one considers that $25,000.00 is the average price of a private university's tuition for one year! Whereas the same courses at Circuit City taught by some of the leading scholars in the country can be bought at a going rate of $14.95 per course or $149.50 for a one-year package of courses in physics, history, accounting, behavioral science, etc., remind me again why I should be paying for the maintenance of a library (we have the public library in town and I am on internet libraries already), for the maintenance of a faculty (I have all of their instructional CDs at home), for the cutting of the grass on campus (I like to go to the public parks, myself), and for the upkeep of the bookstore (I prefer Borders and Barnes & Noble) and the refectory (I prefer Taco Bell and Subway). Why pay the exorbitant tuition when I can buy the CD?

Is it the same old garbage in a brand new dumpster?

So the creative packaging of the collegiate or professional school curriculum becomes the challenge. How to make our outfit look more attractive than their outfit without making it look like we are competing with the publicly traded companies of the world. If we cost more, we must be better, right? Well, when you are selling to eighteen year olds and their eager and naïve parents, then maybe the pretty campus, the big library building, the coffee shop in the campus bookstore, and the football stadium become THE major factors. Never mind the jaded and fatigued tenured faculty. But, when dealing with the seasoned veteran looking for a "real" educational experience, watch out! Packaging is not enough, for this crowd will quickly rip the wrappers off and call a thing by its real name. There is more than one major institution offering "summer institutes" for seasoned professionals through a carefully crafted (the marketing was obviously jobbed out!) marketing scheme in such a way as to simply be recycling the old curriculum from the academic year in shorter doses with compressed teaching by depressed faculty. It seems to work more often than one might suppose, but for how long? Might we look for another and more responsible way of offering doctoral training to the seasoned veteran other than sending them back to the same old boot camp they attended twenty years ago?

Maybe more books, a new gym, guest speakers and a campus coffee shop will help.

I worked for a short time as a consultant to a small evangelical college in the Midwest which had gotten into trouble because of "insufficient library holdings." So being a pragmatist and decidedly not an intellectual, the President went out and bought 20,000 volumes of pulp fiction paperbacks to "boost" the holdings, as he put it. Of course, naturally this didn't exactly make North Central happy and their problems, therefore, persisted. Sometimes, in an effort to keep the doors open (and polished) by way of increasing enrollment and, thus, tuition revenue, academic institutions will reach out to new frontiers of marketing, "institutional development" it is sometimes called, when raising grant money is involved. Buying more books and building new and bigger buildings sometimes helps. Putting in a sports program to attract the collegiate enthusiast is always a possibility. Jazzing up the student center or even the library with new and different culinary options might be explored. And, sometimes, just yelling louder about the institution's merits could help.

Amazon.com and the problem with library hours might be a concern.

Libraries and bookstores on academic campuses are facing more and more problems which too often result in an under-use or misuse of the "learning space." This learning space, i.e., the library, is provided by the college both to hold books to satisfy the accrediting agencies and to impress the parents. For those of us who have lived most of our lives on a college campus and seen the transition of the definition of scholarship erode the virtues of "library retrieval skills," owing to the emergence of the internet libraries, the library has become a "big, expensive study hall and social mixer" for campus living. The internet library never closes, whereas the campus one is usually closed when students are most commonly awake, namely, late night. Also, both the undergraduate and the seasoned veteran can "go to the internet library" in their pajamas, whereas the campus library has a dress code.

Not only that, the internet library has literally millions of full-text books and magazines, and up-to-date e-journals as well, whereas most college and university libraries are constantly struggling to add new titles against a depleting budget. I ask, "Why fight it?" Why not embrace the internet library at the college library and be done with it? If one wishes to "hold a book in the hand," as a sad and disillusioned older librarian said to me recently, then get oneself off to the public library where books which one's own tax dollars have bought can be found aplenty. There, one can hold as many as one likes without it being an expense to the college which, in turn, is passed on to students in tuition charges.

And what about the institution's bookstore? Some of these college bookstores are really sad little closets down the hallway converted into a book store for required textbooks for courses offered on campus. Many of these, of course, are secondhand, tattered but reusable, books leading the small college bookstore to look like an afterthought. Others are very impressive, two or three story affairs with a coffee shop and a clothing store which serves as an alumni self-aggrandizing extravaganza. Here, one can buy pricey books plus a t-shirt while having a latte and bagel thrown into the bargain. Never mind the expense to the student in terms of increased tuition, or the fact that any of the books being sold on campus could be bought at a meager percentage of that cost through Amazon.com's used department. When we have the largest bookstore in the world at our fingertips via the internet, why the mega bookstores on campus? Never mind about the local Borders or Barnes & Noble which outsell everyone and everything! For the seasoned veteran professional returning for the terminal degree while hanging onto their hard-earned position, such things as campus libraries and campus bookstores are a nuisance and a bother.

Do middle-aged professionals really want to play basketball?

And then there is the "Dewey Question." Do we or do we not have a sports program at our institution? This question is important to college presidents who count on alumni giving to keep the doors open. It is important to the college recruiters who are "out there" hunting for the students whom they must attract with something of interest. That wouldn't commonly be the academic merits of the teaching faculty, but something like sports, now, really gets the undergraduates' attention. John Dewey, upon becoming president of the University of Chicago, decided, however, that UC was not about physical fitness and athletic prowess, but rather about scholarship, learning, teaching, researching, etc. He cut his operating budget by millions by scuttling the sports program. Of course, it eventually came back after Dewey was no more, but he made his point.

For the seasoned veteran looking to complete a terminal degree program, the prospects of cheering for the home team loses its savory merits when stacked up against time pressures, money pressures, and professional expectations. Undergraduates, of course, are the market so they determine the agenda, and the sports programs at some institutions have been raised to a

Sacrament!

How much of the tuition goes for the latte dispenser?

Of course, one needs coffee! The question is do we really need a coffee shop in the bookstore? Or the library? Or even on campus? The issues facing academic institutions are convoluted owing to the complex maze of competing interests dictating policy for advancement and development. An institution must have student enrollment in order to have the tuition to pay for the things that assure student enrollment. The stress comes when what is perceived to be needed to attract the undergraduate must be paid for by the graduate student, including the seasoned veteran professional who couldn't care less about the very things that the undergraduates must have in order to even show up on campus.

The problem, it seems, is that academic institutions spread themselves too thinly across too many competing and conflicting markets. The undergraduate (and the concerned parent) may want a big library and beautiful campus, a bookstore with coffee and the sports arena and, thus, the justification for the tuition. On the other hand, the veteran professionals seeking to complete a terminal degree do not need or want any of those things! They want exposure to innovative and creative minds working on the frontiers of their profession, and the possibilities of finding that from a jaded tenured faculty and an expensively maintained cosmetic campus seem less than promising.

At a major university where I held a postdoctoral appointment the budget for maintaining the beautiful campus, the bookstore with a coffee shop, and a landmark library, necessitated exorbitant extortion tuition from students. The tenured faculty was rather settled as well and they often found themselves bringing in "outsiders" to beef up the cutting edge atmosphere of the curriculum. As a matter of fact, many institutions find that only by bringing in the "outside expert" can they stay abreast of the burgeoning fields in which their tenured faculty find themselves teaching. At this university, I came to learn that sports were the tail that wagged the dog, not scholarship, and that the bookstore with its alumni memorabilia was one of the major revenue sources for the institution. It seems that t-shirts and lattes had their rightful place after all!

Will a big speaker bring them on campus or do we need a megaphone?

When trying to attract parents, things like a beautifully manicured campus, an attractive bookstore equipped with a coffee and pastries shop, a spacious student center for socializing, and an impressive library for study hall are all very important. Otherwise, just attend a commuter university, keep the day job, and take an extra semester or year to finish an undergraduate degree for four figures instead of possibly six. For the seasoned professional looking to complete a terminal degree, all of those attractions are really expensive distractions and needless fluff. Yet, the big institutions still tout them as "essentials" of a good education. It might be argued by the disillusioned professional that more real learning at the professional level occurs in adjacent coffee shops and independent second hand bookstores than occurs on such campuses. Combine a lively use of the internet, a good coffee shop, and Amazon.com and you have a winning combination for seasoned professionals seeking to advance their learning in their chosen field.

Karl Marx once said that if an education was what a person really wanted, they should just get themselves a pass card to the British Museum, that is, London's public library. However, up until now, that is, up until the Graduate Theological Foundation came along, there was no really effective way to link those learning mechanisms to a terminal degree. However, rather than raising the volume of the claims to value and merit espoused by some of the leading academic institutions in the country, the Foundation has found that by quietly going along while networking educational venues with professionals seeking advancement, a great deal of learning is happening and it is leading to the desired terminal degree. More on this point in chapter five.

Innovation is just another word for "same ol', same ol'," isn't it?

In dealing with the "old solutions as the Last Dinosaur," we encounter institutions simply trying to polish up the old machine to make it look new, not unlike a detail shop sprucing up clunker cars to look like one-owners. The institutional mindset finds itself in a difficult spot when it does not have the capacity to think outside the box, i.e., institutional self-transcendence. Thus, the institution just keeps on recycling the same old formulas and the same old tired ideas about curriculum and programming. This requires the ratcheting up of the values rhetoric about the institution's programs so the promotional materials look fresh, but the ideas are the same old ideas used generation after generation. Faculty, books, sports, and social life can only be repackaged so many times until repetition becomes normative.

For the seasoned veteran in the professional field of ministry, none of those things seem to matter, for it is not profiling but advanced learning that is the driving force in seeking a terminal degree. And faculty, books, sports, and social life are only important to the extent that they feed that driving force. Whereas the undergraduate is engaged in a desperate attempt to postpone maturity and prolong adolescence, the mature professional seeks desperately to find the cutting edge and learn from it without being caught up in the distractions of an institution's idea about self-promotion.

If we call it by a postmodern name, will that do it?

What we have been suggesting here is that the professional student, with years of experience and a clear vision of what is needed to top off his/her education, should have the right to seek and find that learning experience without paying the price of never actually earning the terminal degree. Yet, if they are restricted to the confines of any specific institution, that felicity of "seek and find" is lost. For the institution, that student becomes essentially a captive until the degree is completed at that institution. The flexibility of finding creative innovators at multiple educational venues may serve the professional student but will not serve the institutional agenda, or so it is thought. So institutions, in an attempt to entice the advanced professional to enroll in their programs, package them according to the perceived market demands and expectations, whether the institution has the capacity or the insight to offer such a program in the first place. It's all about profiling and marketing, it seems, rather than creating a new mechanism to enhance professional learning rather than institutional aggrandizement. Call it "postmodern" and maybe they will come, and stay, and pay, and finish.

When is a requirement not a requirement?

I find it amusing to peruse the literature of major institutions offering terminal degree programs wherein is found a plethora of rules and regulations. Over the years, I have built a veritable library of institutional catalogues precisely to observe this phenomenon. One wonders from where these rules and regulations are derived, especially as they are purported to relate directly to the seasoned professional coming into a program who already holds graduate degrees and years of experience in the field. Who sets the rules, who constructs the regimented process of completing a terminal degree? The faculty? The tenured faculty who have been teaching the same old curriculum year after year, altering just enough to avoid embarrassment? Surely incoming professionals should have jurisdiction over their own degree programs in terms of design, content, execution, etc. If we were dealing with an eighteen year old high school student, then that is one thing, but to use the same formula, the same tired committee, the same visionless disillusioned cadre of faculty to design a doctoral program who also designed a bachelor's program, seems pathetic.

Why not create an educational arena in which incoming professionals design their own programs in terms of content, subject matter, and agenda? Why not let the seasoned professional "fill in the blanks" of a degree rather than "checking off" preset requirements devised by a sitting faculty, a faculty often far removed from the playing field of professional practice? Why have requirements, as such, anyway? Why not have guidelines, parameters, categories of work without dictating the content? Let the professionals make those determinations according to their own best insights into what is needed and wanted for their professional situations. Have a faculty that serves as "consulting colleagues" to the professional student rather than laying down the law, enforcing the rules, and demanding compliance with the preset requirements.

Can certification credit be earned during coffee break?

It seems odd to me to find that learning which occurs at professional associations, training institutes, national conferences, etc., is discounted for degree credit by most graduate programs at universities. Especially when one considers that most of those who are in the leadership position at these associations, institutes, and conferences are themselves graduates of those same universities which fail or refuse to acknowledge the merit of the learning experience at those non-university venues. It seems as though it is an indictment against the institution's own confidence in the quality of training its own graduates can offer.

I remember Robert Frost being asked if he was going to use his own poetry books in a course he was asked to teach at Dartmouth College in poetry. His response was something to the effect of "What kind of a poet would I be that didn't have enough respect for my own work such that I wouldn't use it in the classroom?" Strange that institutions will train advanced professionals who then go out and set up training programs which then their own training institutions refuse to accept.

Over my twenty-two years at the Graduate Theological Foundation, I have seen hundreds of well-trained professionals come to us with an array of distinguished certifications all given by well respected institutions, but leading to no terminal degree. Furthermore, they took their training while keeping their jobs.

How brilliant is that, to continue one's education while keeping the job one would hope to get back after taking the advanced degree. Having it both ways – job and training – is what seasoned professionals really need.

How many certificates equal a degree, anyhow?

And here, of course, is the real dilemma. After an individual has taken the undergraduate degree and the first graduate degree, gets the professional position in which he/she excels and clocks a certain number of years, then the interest comes for a doctorate. Yet, these days one is foolish to walk away from a job that one would hope to get back after taking the terminal degree. So what to do? Simply put, most get themselves off regularly to institutes, conferences, workshops, seminars, all in the process of accumulating certifications and certificates of completion verifying and validating the training they have been taking while keeping their professional employment intact.

Now, how in this scenario is one ever to take a terminal degree? Of course, there are those extremely expensive "distance learning institutions" like Nova and Phoenix, but other than that, what about something realistically related to the certification phenomenon? Why can't those credentials come to something terminal? Why not link a series of preplanned certifications which would lead to a terminal degree? How many certificates, after all, would it take to equal a doctor's degree in a professional field?

Chapter Three

The New Solution

The Student as Client rather than Servant

As we have been saying, there is an imperative for academic institutions to put forth a serious effort to radically differentiate between the undergraduate student (and all that goes with that in terms of program design), and the seasoned veteran professional returning for a terminal degree. To use the same old tired paradigm for program design for both constituencies is folly and has been responsible for a great deal of dissatisfaction among returning professionals. To preset a curriculum and degree program for the eighteen year old is necessary, but it defies reason to use that same mentality in creating a preset curriculum and degree program of sequenced courses for professionals who have been in the field for twenty years and who already hold advanced graduate degrees in cognate disciplines related to their professional practice.

What is called for, of course, is a new solution in the form of a *New Paradigm*. Why treat the returning professional as a student at all? Why not evolve a level type of relationship, a new perception of who they are and what the institution is to them? When institutions employ the same model of interaction for the professional veteran as they use in the care and nurture of the undergraduate, the relationship takes on a kind of surrealism, for the professional veteran is often more informed about the cutting edge of the profession than are the tenured faculty who most often have had little or no experience in the field of practice, and certainly not recently. It's the contract faculty, the adjuncts, the visiting experts, who are usually more informed than the residential faculty.

Therefore, upon the arrival of the seasoned veteran, the relationship must take on a kind of consultative dimension, a collegial interaction, collaboration, and partnership as the fundamental characteristic. This, of course, requires a faculty that is self-confident about its own gifts with a ready willingness to learn from the incoming student-client. A faculty that is defensive about its own lack of experience, having failed to be or to stay in touch with the major advances in their profession, would certainly be off-putting to professionals seeking to advance their academic prowess. But, to alter the relationship to that of a client seeking direction in pursuit of new opportunities, in quest of developing methods to explore the outer reaches of their profession, this should be the provider institution's agenda.

Networking higher education the way multinational corporations do it, right?

This model, this new paradigm of relationship, this completely recast posture of client/institution interaction, then calls for a consciousness-changing experience on the part of both faculty and administrators. No longer will the old cookie cutter modality of faculty/students, students/administration work for these seasoned veterans. The relationship must take on a new reality by acknowledging and affirming the dynamic experience being brought to the learning environment by these veteran clients. Institutions must learn to take advantage of this treasure of experience, to tap into the learned insights of the professional returning from years of practice in the field. Instead of being defensive or intimidated, faculties and institutional administrators should foster, should solicit, should nurture this treasure trove of information, experience, insight, and commitment to the professional field.

Furthermore, the institution that presumes it has all that is being sought by these returning veterans is sadly mistaken, no matter how well equipped its faculty, library, and campus might be. Again, the institution must throw out the old paradigm of the entirely "self-contained" learning environment it employs with undergraduates. Of course, undergraduates need to know that "everything is provided" for their educational needs to keep their comfort level high. But for the seasoned veteran, this notion of a self-contained fully-equipped institution is off-putting because it is unrealistic. This brings up the whole prospect of "networking" the way the corporate world does it, an even more dynamic and creative concept than "outsourcing" components of a preset degree design.

Do I have to buy all of my education from the same place?

This notion of functioning as a "networking system," rather than an enclosed self-contained learning box, will greatly challenge the resilience of the traditional institution, its faculty as well as the administrators. Several factors mitigate against the traditional institution's willingness or even ability to make this transformative redefinition of itself, its programs, and its relationship with the professional student. First, there is the problem of the accounting office, the Bursar's Office, if you will. To defend the idea that an institution will regularly rotate professional students out to other educational venues which, by definition, are not revenue-producing to the home institution, is anathema! Yet, if the institution is to "serve the client's best interest" in providing and/or locating just the right educational and learning experience, it must be willing to "give up" control of the professional student and become a facilitator of that professional's own educational destiny.

In addition to embracing a radical philosophy of collaborative education in facilitating the professional student's own perceived destiny, the faculty must take the bitter pill of acknowledgment that it is not omniscient, or that it is not the be-all of the professional veteran being pursued. A faculty worth its salt, of course, is a faculty that not only knows what it knows, but knows what it doesn't know. And, further, knows those who do know what it itself does not know. This is called being informed in the profession. For the undergraduate faculty-student relationship, it serves both well for there to be this perceived notion of the all-knowing resident faculty. For the professional student, this image is both naïve and off-putting, for both parties, faculty and professional student, know better. Why then attempt to keep up the charade? Why not be forthcoming with information regarding the limitations of the present learning environment, however good it might really be, and then facilitate the student who is seeking to do a specialized bit of training which can certainly be gotten elsewhere, but not here?

Finally, there is the inevitable pressure on the administration of any institution to create an environment of openness about strengths and limitations of the home institution. To know what one's institution is good at and can do well is quite splendid. What is even better is to know the limitations of the home institution's faculty, library, etc. And, furthermore, to also know the educational terrain sufficiently well as to be able to identify where the deficiencies of the home institution can be made up. For an Ivy League institution to direct a professional student to another educational venue to pick up the needed specialization is a sign of strength, not weakness, and a demonstration of legitimate commitment to the education of the professional student, not a sign of disloyalty to the home institution.

Of course, what is being suggested here is that the really effective institution -- its faculty and administration -- is genuinely on top of educational opportunities and advancements being made in the relevant field around the country and around the world. Being in touch, being informed, keeping abreast, all of the things that make an institution a really great institution but a characteristic that is,

40

alas, seldom found and never applauded. If the home institution is unable to meet the needs of a particular professional student, then send that student to the proper educational venue. And this can be done without terminating the student, but rather providing a collaborative mechanism so that the student benefits and both providing institutions, the home institution and the specialized institution, will likewise benefit.

Does any of my professional experience really count?

This brings up another touchy subject with traditionalist institutions, namely, what to do with the professional experience of the veteran student who comes for a terminal degree. Unfortunately, during my twenty-two years as President of my own institution, I have come to learn that the most common, almost knee-jerk, response of the traditionalist institutions to the question is to "ignore" the incoming veteran's experience as much as possible. So instead of integrating the twenty years or so of professional field experience into the overall degree plan, the institution sidesteps that experience by simply providing a roster of graduate courses needed to complete the terminal degree. I have over the years collected horror stories related to this phenomenon, that is, institutional blindness to the gifted incoming professional's experience and potential contribution to the learning environment.

In some ways, this phenomenon raises the issue of an "integrity void" on the part of the institution and its faculty. I have known of professional veterans returning to an institution for the terminal degree in a field in which they had been practicing successfully for a good number of years only to find themselves required to take a course in that specialization from a faculty person who had essentially no practical experience in it! When institutions have enough self-confidence in their own abilities to provide and foster learning at the professional level, then they will be able to move away from a moribund confidence level to a genuine partnership with the student-client in developing and monitoring an individualized study plan designed in consultation with the

41

student and in fulfillment of the student's own personally perceived professional needs and aspirations.

Too often at this professional level of training, the faculty perceives the doctoral student as an instrument of their own making and for their own use. How often do professional students in this situation find themselves "living the dream" of the supervising faculty person instead of pursuing their own dream, doing their own chosen research, writing their own book? I can't count the number of times I have seen professional students come to my institution with horror stories related to this phenomenon of faculty domination over study topic, work agenda, and writing tasks. This happens at the undergraduate level probably more often than it should, but that it happens at all at the postgraduate professional level is a disgrace to the profession of graduate teaching and to institutions that tolerate, indeed, in some instances, encourage such imperialistic subjugation of the professional veteran to the role of a student/servant working at the behest and to the advantage of the supervising faculty.

I really want to do this but will it count for anything?

Frequently, we see that professional veterans returning to pursue a terminal degree learns upon arrival that their heart's desire in terms of study does not fit within the operating model or program definition of the home institution. Thus, either leaving or adjusting one's own plans to suit the institution seem to be the only options. If institutions can let go of the supervisory model of scripted degree design and allow the seasoned veteran participate, even lead, in the tailoring of a personal plan of study, both institution and student-client would be the beneficiaries. Again, we are not speaking of the uninitiated undergraduate in need of spoonfeeding, but rather of a seasoned professional who more often than not knows better than the sitting faculty what is needed, what is wanted, what will prove to be the most beneficial in the practice of the profession for himself/herself. For faculty to become *consulting colleagues* is the aim rather than dictating *pontificators* spouting out the rules and regulations, disregarding the individual needs of professional students. Faculty as colleague and student as client is the model of the New Paradigm. It provides a mechanism whereby educational venues are judged meritorious on the basis of the quality and relevance of their offerings within an arena where a faculty person serves as a consultant, albeit learned in the field, to the student, who is really a client in search of good advice about educational options in the realization of a personal and professional ambition.

My package is great but it doesn't really look like a meal-deal.

The looming phenomenon of the cookie-cutter educational program often stifles the professional in the field from ever actually considering returning for the terminal degree. Just the thought of "jumping through hoops" to satisfy an institutional set of regulations or a faculty making demands about a field in which it is itself inexperienced or out of touch is off-putting to the really creative professional ambitious about the field of practice. A Meal-Deal is not that for which most creative professionals are looking. Rather, the idea of an educational smorgasbord wherein the professional student-clients are at liberty to create just the program of study at just the right places to suit their own personal needs and ambition is what is truly attractive. Why follow some obscure faculty committee's monstrously constructed preset degree program when the professional student-client knows what is needed and, more often than not, the various places where it can be gotten?

An educational shopping mall rather than a Wal-Mart approach will prove more attractive to the ambitious professional. Rather than being stuck in one store, one institution, one set of faculty with one set of rules and regulations, why not allow the student to graze the field, to search and seize the experiences most desired and needed? Instead of the faculty setting all of the limits or the institution establishing the hard and fast parameters, why not let students loose upon the educational playing field to find and package their own degree program? Institutions may provide the framework, but let the student-clients in the professional fields determine the contents. Student-initiated, tailor-made degree programs will be, and are becoming, the reality of the future. There are too many options, online and around the world, for any institution to make the preposterous presumption that it can provide all. This whole approach being suggested here as the New Paradigm, as has already been mentioned, requires a completely new way of thinking about serving the professionally seasoned veteran student not looking for a pretty campus, a library of books, or a distinguished but intransigent faculty. The model is different, the paradigm is radical, the concept of genuine multi-institutional collaboration is the goal.

Do I really have an educational portfolio?

The notion that the incoming professional student, rather than given a roster of preset courses, is given a developmental portfolio is also radical. From a predetermined curriculum designed by nameless faculty in the distant past to an educational portfolio into which the student-client must put the relevant learning components shifts the model towards a more client-centrist position and away from an institutional imperialism. This move is required because the seasoned client is not particularly amenable to being told what to study. Rather, he/she is better served by a faculty that serve as consulting colleagues, offering suggestions and advice, making inquiries and exploring options of learning venues. The institution becomes the base-camp out of which the student then travels to the relevant venues for the needed educational components. The student is likewise proactive in the development and subsequent management of the portfolio which is constantly in a state of development and refinement.

In my own institution, of the 375 doctoral professional student-clients who come to us, half are certain about what their doctoral dissertation topic will be. By the end of the first year, over half of those have changed their minds. Not that their minds have been changed by our faculty, quite the contrary. Based upon their learning experience at their own selected venues of

44

education, they have come to realize that their interests have shifted and the topic must change accordingly. This is called dynamic learning and the student-client is in charge of the process and is the beneficiary of the outcome. Yes, these students do have an educational portfolio which they have been primarily involved in developing and who likewise must be responsible for managing, in consultation with a faculty who serve as veteran colleagues in the field of study being pursued. *Faculty as collegial companion* rather than dominating mentor, creates an entirely different and more nurturing dynamic in the overall interpersonal relationships of the learning environment.

Can I go shopping for educational program opportunities?

Thanks to the internet, educational shopping has become a national pastime. To go online and search the world for just the right place to pursue just the right subject at a time and at a cost that is feasible for the working professional is a new reality; its time has come. What has not happened, by and large, is a concomitant reciprocating response from educational institutions which are still busily marketing their own wares oblivious to the wares being marketed by comparable institutions. Rather than collaborate in the open light of day, they compete in the myopic darkness!

When I was a child, we went to town and went from store to store buying the products that each store specialized in with no expectation of comparative shopping. One bought what was laid out on the shelves or did without. So collegiate education was presented in the same fashion. We have what we have and that's all that we have. Not so anymore. One goes to the shopping mall where there are five shoe stores to choose from and three pharmacies to selectively patronize. And the same should be true of advanced professional education. Why shouldn't professionals be able to go online, find the various educational components needed to complete their overall educational aspirations from several different educational venues and then receive a terminal degree for the effort?

My experience has shown that when these professionals are given such liberty, such jurisdiction over their own educational portfolio, they more often than not go well above and beyond the commonly expected level of professional performance in the completing of the degree program. It has to do with "trusting the consumer," having confidence in the quality of work desired to be done in the final stages of educational formation. Rules and regulations, preset curricula and performance hoops speak volumes regarding the kind of person being pursued by these traditionalist educational institutions. To rely upon the integrity of the student-clients and to hold them to a level of educational performance befitting their profession is an entirely different way of dealing with professionals in the field of practice.

What about packaging to suit my own professional needs?

Dell and Gateway Computers as well as the Saturn automobile company were among the first manufacturers to jump on the idea that the consumer is the boss and to cater to the consumer's personally articulated needs would be a great marketing idea. Then, the investment firms began to market their services in terms of "personalizing" their relationship such that the client becomes a partner in the decision making process, what to buy, when to buy, how much to buy, etc. Today, given the inexhaustible range of professional education available around the world and at home and so readily accessible via the internet, there is a growing expectation among professional student-clients that they might be able to put together a litany of educational components on their own that would lead to a terminal degree. This is not distance learning, but educational venues to which they might have access and then for which they might receive doctoral-level credit. Unlike the undergraduate consumer who really doesn't know what to buy, the seasoned veteran student-client is often more informed about what is needed and where it might be gotten than are faculty and administrators.

At my institution, we have established formalized relationships with many nationally and internationally distinguished educational training institutions, conferences, research and training institutes, etc., from which our doctoral students may select the desired component. They are likewise at liberty to identify educational venues on their own as appropriate to their own professional needs. Dozens of examples from my twenty-two years come to mind. One such illustration is that of a counselor in private practice who expressed a desire to take some specialized seminars at the Cape Code Institute in Massachusetts. We did not know about this outstanding program, so following the investigation in which we learned it was an endeavor in post-credentialed clinical counseling education sponsored by the Einstein College of Medicine at Yeshiva University in New York, well, of course, we validated the Institute and have subsequently sent many students to take part of their educational training there.

Responsive reciprocity is an integral requirement in this process of collaborative education. If Circuit City doesn't have it, maybe Best Buy will, and the more forthcoming with this information on the part of the clerical staff the better for the consumer as well as for the provider. Since there are no secrets anymore about educational programming, thanks to the internet, the more openly informative and willingly reciprocal with information, the better for all concerned. The worst possible posture for any serious educational institution is to presume that if we don't have it, the student doesn't need it! Or, that a concocted alternative will do just as well. It may work on the eighteen year old, but not on the seasoned practitioner.

Can someone tell me what this experience is worth, to me or to them?

One of the most important characteristics of this new paradigm of collaborative education for the seasoned professional is the capacity to know what the current educational terrain offers in all cognates of the professional field being pursued. This, of course, calls for a vigorous and unrelenting commitment to the concept of collaboration, a commitment which necessitates the facilitating institution (the institutional manager of the professional student's portfolio) constantly updating its awareness of existing and emerging opportunities for study, new educational venues, new programs, etc.

Also, the host institution of the student-client portfolio must engage in a systematic, analytical assessment of each of these new and emerging programs as they come along. These pro-active hosting institutions must seek out ways of engaging the new programs from a plethora of institutions such that the student-client may have quick and ready access to them without a lot of inter-institutional red tape. Few things are more frustrating to the student-as-client at the highest professional level than the often required wrestling with the cumbersome administrative hoops. These barriers seldom have any direct bearing on the value and merits of an educational experience, but are put in place by administrators too often for self-validation.

To find the existing and developing programs wherever they are, assess them, establish inter-institutional affiliations with their hosting institutions, and then make these educational venues available to the professional student-client, constitutes the required direction of the future for institutions offering advanced training in cognate fields of ministry. This is the primary function of the new paradigm of collaborative education. Gone are the days, thanks to the internet and the globalization of educational consciousness within the professions, when a single institution could ever legitimately purport to "offer all that is needed" in the final training programs of advanced professionals seeking terminal degrees. *Collaborate* is the mandate of the new paradigm...

The evaluation and validation processes become a crucial responsibility of the faculty and the administrative staff of this forward-looking host institution in its management of the professional student-client's portfolio. A careful, objective, open-minded consideration of the depth and quality of educational experiences being offered by a range of not just academic institutions but offered by professional associations, national conferences, research and training institutes as well, is imperative. Creativity in the evaluation and innovative ideas in the offering of these cutting-edge educational experiences is that for which we are calling. Thanks to globalization and the World Wide Web, we are only limited by our imagination. The establishment of criteria of merit, standards for evaluation, etc., is the domain of the portfolio-managing institution and here the best of the institution's faculty and administrators must step forward and become actively engaged in the process.

Can my educational consultant manage my educational portfolio?

The really seasoned professional will want to know if the host institution is actually prepared, both philosophically and emotionally, to engage in a collegial and collaborative development and management of an educational portfolio. Gone are the days, of course, of rosters ticked off to secure the final degree. Gone are the days when the faculty simply dictates the curriculum and the compliant student, however advanced in training and experience, complies or leaves. Gone are the days when the administration of an institution simply exercises a unilateral domination of the rules and regulations governing an advanced degree program. "Collaborate!" is the battle cry of this newly emerging paradigm of collaborative education. As with financial investment companies trying to attract and hold on to new investors, the collegial-based collaborative institution seeking to attract and maintain the seasoned professional looking to complete a terminal degree must demonstrate by word and deed its willingness and ability to assist in the development of an educational portfolio which is exciting, challenging, innovative, and achievable. If this is done, confidence will be high on the part of both parties, the host institution and the student-client, that the educational goals can and will be met.

49

Are the Key Master and the Gate Keeper in cahoots?

One of the greatest challenges institutions face, which are attempting to embrace and implement this new paradigm of collaborative education, is to convince the seasoned veteran would-be student-client that the institution is truly committed to this new and radical philosophy of post-credentialed education. The suspicion that the program is merely old garbage in a new dumpster must be dispelled. The Key Master cannot conspire with the Gate Keeper when it comes to the highest levels of professional education, that is, the host institution must see its loyalty and commitment to rest with the student-client and not with other host institutions that likewise stand to benefit from collaboration. Programs at other educational venues must be assessed objectively and fairly, with no hint of mutuality of benefit in the collaboration at the expense of the student's own education. The world of politics is fraught with just such collaborative conspiracies and the educational world must steer clear of any taint of such self-serving activity.

Who has the right to say what is valuable and why?

When it comes to the assessment process, it seems to me that it is crucial for the integrity and credibility of the host institution to provide a mechanism whereby the student-client, as seasoned professional, has the opportunity to participate. It seems ludicrous for a sitting faculty, possibly tired and too often prematurely tenured, to take upon itself the sole responsibility and right to assess and evaluate educational venues from around the country and around the world. Since these newly emerging educational venues, we are arguing, should and must count towards the terminal degree, and are often and increasingly being offered in the non-university arena of professional education, university faculties may actually be the least qualified to do the assessments and evaluations.

Seasoned veterans, the one who have been in professional practice for twenty years and who have kept up with, and are aware of, the educational innovations occurring in their cognate fields of learning, are the individuals who should have a central role in the evaluation process. From these practicing professionals in the field, the merits of an educational venue can rather quickly receive a fair and reasonable assessment of its merits. Unlike the self-protecting and ever-doubting traditionalist on the faculty who may have little clue as to the value of an educational program as relates to the practice of the profession, having been so long absent from its day-to-day demands, the professional student-client is Johnny-on-the-spot.

When is a credit not a credit and what does a debit mean in education?

The emergence in this country of the "credit system" of education has a fascinating and convoluted history. Unlike the European system, we assess learning on the basis of earned credits rather than demonstrated competency by way of existing examinations. At Oxford University, where I have been teaching in the international summer program for a number of years, the student must take tutorials and occasionally attend a university lecture, but the degree earned must be done so on the basis of a comprehensive examination administered after three years of residence. Never mind the grades or courses taken in the interim for there is no cumulative transcript. In the U.S., we want the student to accrue credits, sort of like a savings stamp program. So after you have accumulated a certain specified number of particular types and kinds of credits, you get a degree. In the U.S., we offer degrees by earned credits rather than by demonstrated competency and, thus, we have many people with degrees but fewer with actual skills.

We have, most unfortunately, carried over this idea from the undergraduate to the graduate degree programs as well, simply adding more courses with bigger numbers to indicate "advanced" offerings. The end result is we have many people wearing terminal degrees who have been educated beyond their intelligence, but if one has accumulated the credits, one must receive the degree. In Europe, the advanced degrees are based upon scholarly performance in the writing of a thesis or dissertation, nothing more, and the ability to successfully defend the end product before a committee of seasoned scholars in the relevant field of research. This is graduate education at its best, not a credit system of stamp collecting whereby most people with the tenacity of a bulldog can eventually get the desired degree, irrespective of scholarship or intelligence.

As with debit and credit cards in the market place, higher education in the U.S. has become a system of deposits and withdrawals. The new paradigm of collaborative education attempts to move beyond this mercantile notion of "components for sale" to a more interactive collaboration between the student-client (not as consumer but as colleague) and the host institution (not as the retail market place but as collaborator).

If it is valuable to me, may I count it?

The new paradigm of collaborative education attempts to stand the evaluation process on its head, namely, by looking to the seasoned professional as the primary grid of program evaluation rather than an institutional faculty or administration. We have been arguing cogently that veterans in from the trenches of their profession are nearly always more prepared to make a fair and accurate assessment of the educational merits of a particular training or learning venue than are the faculty and administration of a host institution. Such being the case, the host institution will serve well its student-clients as well as itself by drawing these seasoned veterans into the assessment and evaluation process. This is particularly the case where the student-clients have identified educational venues which are attractive and relevant to their own developing portfolio.

No faculty or administration has the time or the know-how to continually search the educational terrain for every conceivably beneficial learning experience to offer its student-clients. Whereas often the seasoned professional, or so it has proven to be

52

during my twenty-two years of higher education, is the very person to look to for advice regarding existing and emerging programs and their overall value and merit for a terminal degree program. And, if assessed by the student-clients as being of merit and of particular value to their educational portfolio, then the host institution would be wise to acknowledge and validate the venue for credit. In other words, if doctoral student-clients think it is of worth to their own educational aspirations, that should be the litmus test for acceptance, rather than some arbitrary set of criteria created by a faculty committee working in the abstract.

Why is what I like not enough?

The inevitable question posed by the seasoned veteran to the sitting faculty is just to the point of the new paradigm in collaborative education. Who is to decide, after all? The veteran in the trenches or the faculty in the tower? The institutional administrator busy balancing demands from the Bursar's Office for fiscal responsibility and pressure from the faculty to increase enrollment? When institutions have enough self-confidence in their ability to identify and accept innovative responsible doctoral students who have years of experience in their relevant fields of ministry, those institutions will be prepared to rely upon those same veterans to participate in the development of collaborative relationships with many different types of educational venues worthy of doctoral study. On the other hand, when professionals in the field see such institutions validating both their own field experience and creatively engaging in collaboration with other types of educational venues, then they will return to those host institutions to pursue their own advanced studies, not as students deferring to faculty, but as colleagues collaborating with likeminded scholars in the overall pursuit of quality post-credentialed education.

Chapter Four

Shifting a Paradigm in a
Time of Transition

Shifts in consciousness have marked the evolution of human development, and in some ways the "history of ideas" is the hallmark of the human animal. The major shifts in human consciousness, in self-perception, in the emergence of new ways of seeing reality, all bespeak an imperative for advancement, a drive to improve, and will to meaning. Henry Ford and the automobile, Lewis and Clark and the Northwest Passage, and John and Charles Wesley and their redefinition of the Christian religion, all bespeak of paradigm shifts.

Of course, the old paradigms continue in some form or another even after the breakthrough into new modes of insight occurs. But to presume that higher education and the training of professionals today is the way it has always been is naïve and foolish. The present university model in America is barely three hundred years old, if that, and prior to its emergence, other models existed such as the apprentice model and the guild. Arguments can still be made for the effectiveness of apprenticeships, and instances of its survival in the new methodologies of education still exist, for example, with the internship programs of medical schools, law schools, and divinity schools.

It seems to me that another shift is occurring. Not that we will leave behind and in the dust the old model, but that another methodology, a new approach, a pioneering response to the emergence of new technologies and globalization of consciousness has necessitated a more adventurous address to the advanced ongoing training of ministry professionals. Of course, we need self-contained graduate institutions; of course, seminaries will continue to do what they do best, viz., training the clergy for pastoral ministry. Yet, with the rapidly accelerating diversification of definitions of ministry, far beyond the realms of parish ministry, the necessity for other modes of learning, other paradigms for training, other concepts of venue creation, selection, and validation has become absolutely mandatory.

"The old model worked, once," said Henry Ford.

We have taken a cold, hard look at the traditionalist institution which purports to offer advanced post-credentialed training for the seasoned veteran professional and have found it wanting in several ways. These institutions too often find themselves rearranging chairs on the Titanic by attempting to be creative in the old paradigm – coffee shops in the bookstore, off-campus courses in Wal-Mart and the local hospital, more sports, more books, etc., all of which bespeak an awareness that all is not well in this field of advanced education. The continued utilization of the undergraduate model of faculty/student, student/ administration relationships cannot be forced upon this mature set of practitioners who have returned to the institution seeking a terminal degree. Wishing not to be treated as a college student, these professionals seek to be affirmed and nurtured in their own pursuit of an advanced educational opportunity which they themselves have been actively involved in creating.

Those seeking to be professional must come to us.

This notion that the institution has put in place everything needed for the advancing professional's on-going education is ludicrous.

No matter how sophisticated the institution's facilities, distinguished its faculty, or up-to-date its library and bookstore, no institution can presume to offer everything needed for the complete development of the professional seeking a terminal degree. At most, the institution can hope to offer a hosting environment in which professional student-client can receive direction, encouragement, and collaboration in the development of their own personalized portfolio of educational opportunities.

Those seeking to be professional must learn and study here.

In the new paradigm of postgraduate, post-credentialed professional education, a full acknowledgment and accounting of the central place the internet plays must be boldly articulated. We cannot presume anymore that the internet with all of its globalization-enhancing dynamics is a cute little addendum to the tried and true faculty-developed, administration-driven curriculum and degree program. The invention of movable type and the emergence of the automobile radically transformed the meaning and nature of the educational process, and the same can be said today in terms of the World Wide Web. Those institutions which fail to realize and recognize the educationally-enhancing potential of the internet are rapidly being left behind. Where is "here" in a World Wide Web world? At this moment, my institution has over seventy-five professionals completing their doctoral studies in twenty-nine foreign countries with their access to the tools of learning provided by the internet. So whether they are in Cairo or Chicago, Paris or Philadelphia, is more or less irrelevant to their access to research materials needed for their studies. "Here" is nowhere or everywhere on the World Wide Web.

Those seeking to be professional must follow our rules.

Regulations and rules set down by a faculty and managed by an administration may work with eighteen year olds (or maybe not), but when it comes to dealing with seasoned veterans who know all about traditionalist education, who hold both undergraduate and graduate degrees, who have been practicing professionals in the field for several years, this traditionalist model of education will not work (and probably never did). What is called for now in the new paradigm is an institutional commitment to "collaboration" with the seasoned student as client in the proactive development of an educational portfolio that the institution can manage and from which the professional student can benefit.

Those seeking to be professional must hold our degrees.

There was a time when holding the right degree from the right place was crucial to get the right job. Thanks to the internet and globalization of professional consciousness, this is no longer the case. Granted, a top professional degree from a top institution is not to be disparaged! Yet, given the level of creativity by a variety of up-and-coming institutions, and in light of the rapidly accelerating distance learning programs and programs built around short-term module educational units, it has become possible for almost any professional to study almost anywhere in the world at any time.

Furthermore, and thanks to the internet, in the absence of expensive campus grooming costs, the absence of the need for a massive physical library, and the emergence of a new phenomenon known as the "contract faculty" which is rapidly replacing the tenured faculty at many leading centers of learning, exorbitant educational costs are no longer required defensible, or tolerable. The terminal degree no longer assures an individual of a certain position of employment, for terminal degrees have become a standard requirement, or at least an expectation, within most professions – medicine, law, education, ministry. The carrot is no longer just the terminal degree itself but the prospect of actually "learning something new and helpful in one's profession" is the driving force behind advanced education-seekers.

No one in any of the major professions would disparage the

terminal degree when it has now become the great expectation of all of the traditional professions. What one must now control are costs, timetable for study, and location of educational venues. There needs to be a collaborative component in which the student-as-client can participate, even lead, the development of an educational plan leading to a terminal degree worthwhile, that is to say, relevant to the professional veteran expending time, energy, and resources to secure it.

The history, for example, of the Doctor of Ministry in the professional field of pastoral work is fascinating within itself. As I learned several years ago from Krister Stendahl during an appointment at Harvard University, the early 1960s saw experiments which proved unsuccessful in the divinity schools' attempts to keep abreast with the medical and law schools in offering a terminal professional degree in ministry for pastors. One of the major obstacles to the eventual development of the Doctor of Ministry which has now become the standard mark of completed ministry education, was the faculties and administrations of the divinity schools themselves. These faculties and administrators had worked so long with the Ph.D. as the model of doctoral studies that the D.Min. became in their regimented world nothing more than a "little Ph.D." Thus, the absence of any sense that the profession could itself have a doctorate addressed to its needs, its responsibilities, its uniqueness, a really "professional doctorate" rather than "merely an academic doctorate." It finally worked and now is the standard for professional excellence.

"There must be another way," said Lewis to Clark.

It's not enough to continue to do the same old thing the same old way, especially in advanced professional education, for the terrain is forever changing, shifting, and adapting. It's not just that the content of a profession is forever growing, redefining itself, rethinking its agenda, etc., but that methods of learning are changing exponentially. No longer will the most creative and dynamic professional student-client be quite satisfied with the "talking head." Odd, I find it, that even with the knowledge we now have, thanks to Piaget and others, of effective pedagogy, which says that the lecture is the least effective mechanism available in the learning process, that even the leading schools of education at our major universities still use the "talking head" pedagogical methodology most of the time! It's like calling attention to the indispensable invention of the telephone in communication while still insisting upon using the smoke signal method for daily communication. It is astounding to me to know, first hand, that even a course in innovative pedagogical methodology is being taught in a lecture format!! Again, it's like offering a course in video technology without ever using a camera. I often hear of faculty who still place "on reserve in the library" relevant documents for a course they are teaching rather than making it available via the internet. It is as if there is educational value and learning virtue in making students "go to the library" when one can rightfully ask, "Where and why is the library at all?"

In an internet world, where is "here" and "there"?

This issue, of course, brings to the fore all we have been saying about "where is here and there," anyway? What's the use of the internet if geopolitics still dominates the educational terrain? Why does anyone have to be anywhere in order to take advantage of learning opportunities? Especially if those who are potential learners are themselves advanced professionals practicing in the field. There is an old joke famous with George Jessel that goes something like this: A man comes home late at night and goes into his bedroom where his wife is already in bed and as he opens the closet door to hang up his clothes, there stands a naked man who shrugs and says, "Everybody's gotta be somewhere." It was true once, but now we wonder. Do I really have to be anywhere at any given time? Might I make time and space virtual in order to fit my schedule? We all have the experience of emailing friends and colleagues around the world, often not even knowing where they actually "are" at any given time of communication. Furthermore, educational opportunities are to be had any time, any place. For an institution to presume that its professional student-clients are going to be "on campus" and "on time" is ridiculous and flies in the face of advancing technologies and global consciousness.

In an internet world, is knowledge in a book or on the web?

Recently I heard a distinguished elderly colleague at Oxford say, "It's no longer how or where you find it but what you find that's important in scholarship." What a radically different notion of scholarship than just a few years ago. In an earlier, less technologically complex world, the academy was the seat of learning, faculty, and books. And, the best faculty knew the best books, and, what's important for scholarship, knew how to use them. Shuffling off to the library, briefcase in hand, determination marking the face, and dedication dictating the pace, scholars spent their days strolling up and down the aisles of the repository of printed knowledge ever searching for new insights. "The library," said Alfred North Whitehead once upon a time, "is from where we all should be." The little story, encapsulated here, is that upon one occasion at a faculty cocktail party at Harvard, younger faculty were introducing themselves around by saying, "I'm from Theology, I'm from Biology, I'm from Literature." One colleague, a staff librarian rather than faculty, simply introduced himself as "I'm just from the library," to which, it is said in the hagiography of the Harvard Faculty Club, Whitehead was heard to pipe up and say rather loudly, "From which all of us should be!"

No longer can we make that simple assumption. I know of any number of outstanding undergraduates as well as distinguished professionals who never darken the doors of the campus library but are, nonetheless, on the cutting edge of their discipline. No longer can we assume that the righteous are those who go to church but, like Emily Dickinson once said, "Some keep the Sabbath by going to church, I keep it by staying home." Some do their work in the library on campus, but more and more of the cutting-edge professionals are doing their work by staying home, on the web. Once scholarship was defined by who knew how to find what they needed in the library and quickly. Today any twelve year old has at his/her fingertips the scholarship of the world in full text at any time or place desired. It's now more and more what you do with what you have that makes the difference.

With electronic libraries and the internet, what does "residency" really mean?

No one is saying books are a thing of the past, whether printed or e-books! What is being questioned here is the old-fashioned notion that good scholarship must be radiated from the physical library on the university campus. Access to the physical books seems no longer to be directly correlated with the integrity of the study. Indeed, regional accrediting agencies are finding themselves in a real muddle in trying to sort out the differences, the real differences, the differences that make a difference in learning and education, between the internet full-text library and the campus library.

To require a university to have x-number of actual books on the shelf in order to receive certain kinds of accreditation seems absolutely unreal in the modern age. Archaic is the mindset that correlates physical books with learning and with education. It's the content, the information, what is found therein that is important. It's like suggesting that what is written in a letter is more real and valuable than what is said on the phone!!! Phones and letters or books and internet, it all comes to the same thing. Information is the key, not the medium in which it is found. And I say this as one who has a huge personal library and who served as a Senior Editor of a scholarly publishing house for twenty-five years. Somewhere amongst Amazon.com, the public library, and Borders Bookstore there is a need for a college library, but that need, thanks to these three pillars of learning, is a much smaller need than in bygone days.

In the absence of employment, is a degree an asset or a liability?

When it comes right down to it, there are legitimate arguments these days against taking the degree before actual employment commences. In some instances, a growing number of instances, the workplace wants to be involved in the training of the new recruit rather than having someone come in with a degree which, by implication, demands more money but still requires the same amount of training. Having the new recruits prior to graduation and letting them learn on the job while finishing their formal education seems to be the practice of more and more companies these days. It is not unusual in the workplace today to see individuals turned away who are "overeducated," cases in which having the advanced or terminal degree becomes a debit rather than a credit. Even in the public school systems of America this is a common practice, viz., spurn the master's degree holder and take the bachelor's degree teacher who can be paid less and, within the system, gradually and incrementally earn the master's and maybe the doctorate.

Within the professions, the advanced degree, and particularly the terminal degree, is no longer immediately sought upon completing the undergraduate degree, but rather following ordination or the certification process in counseling, etc. The practitioners are commonly finding that several years into the profession is a better time to pursue the terminal degree. In the "olden days," many of us went straight through – B.A., M.A., M.Div., Ph.D. and launched ourselves in our late twenties. It worked, or at least it worked for some of us. I found, however, that my education was not complete even after taking the Ph.D. at twenty-seven. So I went after postdoctoral appointments at top schools and finally and eventually completed my institutional education.

Today, the process is different and better, it seems to me. Many younger professionals, those with the Master of Divinity degree and holding ordination, are finding that selected certification programs in specialized fields of ministry serve them very well in terms of professional advancement. The terminal degree then comes later, after being established, after accumulating a plethora of praxis-based certifications. What we are suggesting here in the new paradigm is that the accumulation of these certifications might and should actually be leading to the earning of a professional doctorate. Why spend years accumulating highly-specialized certifications from leading educational venues – institutes, conferences, centers – only to have to go back to the traditionalist institution to take all of the requirements for a terminal degree? Why not cluster the certificates in such a fashion that they themselves indicate terminal degree status?

"Hey, I think I've found a New Method," said John to Charles.

When John and Charles Wesley at Christ Church College in Oxford University began to experiment with a formula approach to piety, they were teased about their new "method," and thus "Methodism" was born and subsequently became one of the leading Protestant churches in the world. When Henry Ford hit upon the idea of putting together vehicles on a moving belt with stationary workers, he was teased as well. However, both Methodism and Ford Motor Corporation have faired well, thanks to a New Method. And, such might just be the case with post-credentialed professional education.

Bringing together the reality of the internet and the globalization of consciousness such that the seasoned veteran professional student-client can integrate both access to unlimited information via the World Wide Web and take advantage of short-term educational venue experiences of the highest caliber, is the New Method emerging in higher professional education today. To deny it is to defy reality and to stand in the face of inevitability.

64

Why not acknowledge professional experience as real, true, and good?

Often, with traditionalist institutions, there has been the blatant and recalcitrant unwillingness to acknowledge any "outside" experience as of any real relevance to the securing of the terminal degree. Rather, the expectation is that, when even seasoned veteran professionals show up on campus to commence doctoral studies, they are a *tabula rasa*, a blank tablet, without insight, without experience, without ability and, therefore, it resides with the tenured faculty to teach them what they need to know.

This mentality, all too prevalent though often either denied or unacknowledged, is simply unacceptable. If anything, the institution and its faculty should welcome the returning veterans as major sources of insight and information, of experience and vision. What once was called "life experience" and was given, ever so reluctantly, some academic credit towards an undergraduate degree by, frequently, the less savory academic institutions of the country, should now and at this level be acclaimed as a major component of the overall relationship of the veteran student as client to the host institution. Rather than spurning the professional experience brought onto campus in the form of a lively practitioner, this lively practitioner should be embraced, held up, and utilized in the ongoing development of new programmatic designs of terminal degrees which really address the issues of the day.

Why not let the student identify his/her goals, ambitions, dreams?

We have argued before for the central role professionally seasoned students should play in the development of their own educational portfolio. How highhanded, narrow-minded, and overbearing is the notion that the tenured faculty sitting amidst the ivy and the coeds could, should, or would have the ability to design just the right program for the incoming seasoned veteran.

For the undergraduate badly in need of guidance, certainly, let the faculty be as highhanded and overbearing as they wish and if they must. But when dealing with professionals who have years of experience in the actual practice of what too often is taught by an inexperienced and badly out of practiced faculty who enjoys the comfort and protection of the ivy-covered walls of the academy, high-handedness is out of place.

One of the dangers of an institutionally-driven faculty advising process is that, too often at the doctoral level, the teaching faculty have themselves agendas which too easily and often unwittingly get foisted off onto the student. Setting the work agenda for the undergraduate seems to be a rightful responsibility of the faculty, but to preempt the creative energy and innovative initiative of the seasoned veteran student is unconscionable. It happens, however, far too often, that incoming doctoral students find themselves writing the papers, doing the research, and engaging in projects not of their own choosing, but which are quietly and insistently laid down by the supervising faculty.

Both the acknowledgment of the goals, ambitions, and dreams of the incoming professional, and the empowerment of that professional to realize them, should be the sole purpose of the institution and its faculty. To facilitate by collaborating in the development of a personalized educational portfolio, to nurture by networking with other educational venues offering different and complementary learning opportunities, and to encourage the realization of one's dreams should and could be the primary driving force of a faculty comfortable with its own strengths as well as shortcomings. Once a doctoral-level faculty moves beyond and above any sense of its own omniscience, at that juncture that faculty becomes truly a responsible and worthy partner in the educating of professionals.

Can I study when I'm able and pay what I can?

Another feature this new paradigm calls for in institutional redefinition is that the faculty move beyond the notion of setting

66

the parameters for learning, establishing a curriculum to be adhered to, and rather move to a self-consciousness about its role as facilitator, nurturer, collaborator, indeed, even cheerleader, to the seasoned professional who has paid the institution a favor by returning for further study. Instead of setting up course titles, times, and prerequisites, the institution must seek to collaborate with students as clients in the development of an educational portfolio that serves the needs and meets the life-demands of the students themselves.

Rather than designing degree programs around the schedules of the institutional staff (like hospitals do for nurses and physicians), the new paradigmatic institution encourages the student to take the initiative in the determination of educational venues to be visited, courses, workshops, seminars to be attended, and, while we are at it, determine the costs of these educational adventures such that when the student completes the degree there is no deep indebtedness (as is today too often the case).

The semester system works, more or less well, for the undergraduate who is usually badly in need of discipline, oversight, and pampering. To require a study regime of rising, washing, eating, studying, socializing, and sleeping is the housekeeping and babysitting chores of the typical residential undergraduate college. The latter function, i.e., babysitting, is directly correlated to the tuition so the higher the tuition the more substantial the babysitting. And, at the end of the day, there is little harm done and sometimes even some good if nothing more than the necessary prolongation of adolescence which allows for a degree of maturity to occur. Not uncommonly, the higher the socio-economic level of the student, the longer the process takes. So it seems not to be surprising that the middle and upper class children take longer to mature than do working class children.

But, when it comes to mature veterans with graduate degrees and years of experience between themselves and adolescence, then the case is entirely different even if academic institutions fail to realize it. To put in place an educational model which allows this type of student to maintain their employment while simultaneously pursuing the terminal degree seems only right and proper. Why should this type of student leave a good paying job to take a terminal degree in two or three years which then, hopefully, would secure them a job like the one they left in the first place? Why not work within the framework of solid employment, indeed, why not let that position constitute a sort of working laboratory for the middle/upper management veteran seeking a terminal degree?

The old paradigm – courses, campuses, tenured faculty, rules and regulations – seems increasingly a thing of the past, a dinosaur which once roamed the land but is now being stifled by the pressures of a new age, a new concept of education, a new modality of learning, a new paradigm of institutional responsiveness to the demands and needs of the professional student. To work with, not against, the system of professional employment these students live in, and to provide quality intensive short-term learning venues which can be accumulated for the earning of a doctor's degree, is the way of the future. That institution which embraces this reality, which sees that collaborative education in a consultative posture relative to the student as client constitutes the inevitability of the coming age, is the sort of institution for which there seems to be a bright future.

The creation of a mechanism which allows for and, indeed, fosters, a wide-ranging roster of educational venues for the pursuit of the terminal degree, there must likewise be informed by the realization on the part of these new paradigmatic institutions that educational costs have, for the most part, gotten completely out of hand. Costs have, in some sense, kept pace with the spiraling and irresponsible health care costs in this country. It is now quite common for the graduating undergraduate to walk across the stage leaving with both a diploma and a burdensome debt comparable to the cost of buying a home. And, for graduating doctoral students – ministry, education, medicine, law, etc. – a student may graduate owing a debt which will for all practical purposes take the duration of their professional life to pay back.

There must be another way for professionals to earn a doctor's degree, designed by them to suit their own professional needs, and still be affordable. By this we mean a reasonable cost for a degree which further advances their career without necessarily implying a greater advancement in income resulting from it.

Am I really free to choose my courses, where I study, and cut my costs?

So what we have been saying in this chapter comes down to this. In the new paradigm of graduate education, a paradigm which responsibly addresses and embraces the internet and globalization of consciousness, the professional veteran as student-client will be in a position to essentially take the lead in the development of a professionalized educational portfolio. This portfolio will network with a variety of learning venues in the country and the World Wide Web such that the terminal degree program constitutes a veritable patchwork of integrated learning experiences designed to speak specifically and personally to the individual needs of the student and not, certainly, to simply adhere to a preset curriculum by an institutionalized faculty.

Furthermore, in addition to setting the limit and range of learning experiences to be accessed, the student as client is, therefore, at liberty to identify the places of learning, realizing, of course, that learning must occur where learning is available and must not be limited to a single campus or a single faculty.

Finally, in the new paradigmatic state of the forward looking institution, the student will, by means of networking various educational venues and experiences in the development of a doctoral studies program, be able to control costs of the experience. If one cannot go to the summer program in theology at Oxford University to take an especially attractive seminar or to the Centro Pro Unione in Rome or the Jung Institute in Zurich, then one must look closer to home. This shopping around for competing and comparable learning venues is greatly enhanced by the internet with which any professional student would be quite at home. Controlling courses, locations, and costs – this is the future in the new paradigm of professional-level education. In the following chapter, we will investigate one such institution which has an established reputation in this new modality of education.

Chapter Five

THE FOUNDATION

Going It Alone Doesn't Work Anymore

Though in the previous four chapters I have occasionally, but by intention sparingly, mentioned my own institution, the Graduate Theological Foundation, I will take an author's liberty to speak specifically and in depth about this institution in this closing chapter. I have been President of the Foundation since 1982 and have seen over 1,500 ministry professionals, laity, religious, and clergy, commence and complete their graduate studies under our care. (Note: In the interest of ease of writing, I will refer to the Graduate Theological Foundation throughout this chapter as simply "the Foundation." During this time, I have held postdoctoral appointments at the University of Chicago, the University of Notre Dame, and at Harvard University as well as regularly teaching in the summer program in theology of Oxford University. Within the Foundation's student body, some thirty-nine countries have been represented and twenty-seven different Christian denominations, all four branches of Judaism (Orthodox, Conservative, Reformed, and Reconstructionist), and three branches of Islam (Sunni, Sufi, and Shiite), not to mention a plethora of "unaffiliated" professionals.

During this time the institution has gone through several incremental transformations, each reflecting a commitment to the emerging new paradigm of professional education. We graduate around fifty students annually and our enrollment has held steady for eighteen years at about 375 professional students, of which nearly 40% are women, 15% are non-US citizens, and 30% are Roman Catholic. Though this chapter is not to be the history of the Foundation, we will draw from our institutional history to demonstrate the evolutionary processes through which we have passed in order to arrive at our present situation.

What will follow will be an explanation of how the Foundation functions now, with only passing reference to its earlier, less developed stages of growth out of which has emerged this new paradigm of professional education. Naturally, some of the alumni/ae have themselves been caught up in the growing pains of evolution and for their patience and participation in this process, the Foundation and I are deeply appreciative. What follows is not, unlike the previous four chapters, a speculative musing about what if, what might be, wouldn't it be nice if, sort of a discussion. What follows will be an in-your-face presentation of what is, how this institution functions, and why.

The Students

A Collaborative Concept

The Foundation does not even presume to go it alone in the educating of professionals. Granted, we have a contract faculty of twenty-two scholars from five countries with international reputations attached to each. And, for the most part, our most distinguished faculty members hold named professorships, named rather than endowed, as a demonstration of the breadth and depth of the Foundation's commitment to scholarship in all quarters of learning. For the most part as well, our faculty either hold present faculty appointments at internationally distinguished institutions or hold emeritus status from such institutions as

Fordham University and Christ Church College at Oxford University. But going it alone, never. With fourteen different religious traditions represented on the faculty (Roman Catholic, Orthodox, Anglican, Methodist, Lutheran, Baptist, Mennonite, Quaker, Church of the Brethren, Orthodox Rabbi, Reformed Rabbi, Sufi, Swedenborgian, and Presbyterian), with most holding clerical status within their respective traditions, the role of the faculty as consultant to the administration and evaluators of student performance is central to the overall operation of the Foundation's degree monitoring and degree granting activities.

It might be helpful here to indicate the nature of responsibility and function of our faculty and administration. Faculty function for the Foundation in four different capacities, viz., (1) evaluators of student performance in the writing of papers for educational experiences, (2) directors of theses and dissertations, (3) collaborators with the administration in the identification and assessment of the educational value of different venues of learning, and (4) tutors as the need and interest arise. Stipends are offered in relationship to each of these functions and each contracted faculty person has the "right of waiver" if he or she is unable to discharge a particular duty.

The recognition of the absolute autonomy and independence of our contract faculty has, over the years, proven to be a very helpful characteristic in assuring the Foundation of maintaining an extremely high level of distinguished scholars on its faculty roster. Some faculty are extremely busy, by choice, while others function only occasionally as the interest and opportunity present themselves.

The administration of the Foundation is in the hands of a small fulltime staff of six officers and four stipendiary staff. The President, Provost, Registrar, Bursar, and Director of Marketing and Publications are fulltime in the home office in Indiana where we have been as an institution since 1982, moving from the Archdiocese of New York where the Foundation began in 1962.

In addition to the senior administrative staff, there is a Dean of Faculty, Dean of the Foundation, Dean of Convocation, and Oxford Liaison Officer. The Dean of Faculty is the senior representative of the faculty and the Dean of Convocation oversees the Convocations and Graduation ceremonies of the Foundation which are especially important activities for a community that is only together on two grand occasions, viz., at the Orientation Session at the beginning of their studies and at the Convocation and Graduation at the end of their studies. Whereas the primary duties of the faculty involve evaluation of institutions and student performance, the administrative staff are responsible for assisting the student in the development of an educational portfolio and the careful monitoring of it throughout the degree process.

The interest on the part of the Foundation is to provide our professional students the widest possible berth in the development and execution of their educational portfolio and, in order to do this, we must look wide and far, close and near, to find just those educational venues of interest and value to our students. Thus, going it alone is never a choice for the Foundation. We collaborate, we consult, we explore, always as a joint venture between student and faculty, client and institution.

In the interest of "not going it alone," the Foundation maintains several levels of relationships with educational institutions and learning centers around the country and around the world. Because the Foundation requires its professional students to choose their educational venues from other institutions, we have found that other institutions, learning centers, research institutes, training facilities, etc., are eager to affiliate with us, thereby assuring themselves of some of the enrollment traffic we inevitably create. Some of these affiliations have resulted in exponential growth of the institutional programs, adding faculty, increasing offerings, etc. A comprehensive listing within the various categories to be mentioned here can be seen on the Foundation's website at www.gtfeducation.org. though the list of affiliations in all categories continues to grow, the website will give some idea of the range of educational opportunities made available to our students owing to our institutional commitment to "not going it alone."

The levels of inter-institutional affiliation include (A) the Special Institutional Cooperation and Collaboration (SICC), the (B) Partnering Resources In Ministry Education (P.R.I.M.E.) Relationship, the (C) Recognized and Endorsed (R & E) Relationship, the (D) Approved Venue Sites (AVS) designation, and the (E) Consultative Ecclesial Bodies.

I mention these and will discuss them briefly in an attempt to demonstrate both the incremental levels of affiliations and their merits as well as suggest the diversity of the Foundation's pursuit of learning environments which will benefit our extremely diverse student body. It should be pointed out here that all of our students are experienced professionals in their fields of ministry – parish life, administration, education, mediation, counseling, sacred music, health care, law enforcement and firefighting, and media and creative arts.

Not going it alone means, finally and genuinely, that the Foundation has determined to identify outstanding educational venues of value to our student-clients and then establish, at one of four levels, recognition of those venues so as to benefit our student-clients as they make their selections in the fulfillment of their degree requirements.

(A) Special Inter-institutional Cooperation and Collaboration (SICC). Only two institutions enjoy this level of relationship and they are Oxford University and the Centro Pro Unione in Rome. With Oxford University's Summer Programme in Theology, the Foundation cooperates and collaborates in the setting of courses and faculty; Foundation students have immediate access to the summer program as their needs and interests might dictate. The Foundation sends on average fifty or so doctoral students annually to Oxford University and, in turn, Oxford University faculty serve on the faculty of the Foundation.

The Director of the Oxford University Summer Programme in Theology is a member of the University's theology faculty and holds a named professorship at the Foundation. The Centro Pro Unione in Rome is the educational and research study center which houses all of the relevant documents in ecumenical studies from both the Vatican and the World Council of Churches. It is maintained by the Franciscan Friars of the Atonement (the Greyfriars of New York) and the Director is both a member of the faculty at the Angelicum and holds a named professorship at the Foundation.

(B) The P.R.I.M.E. institutions are those which have in place a comprehensive educational program evaluated by the Foundation at a level such that all of the required Units of Study for our doctoral degrees can be taken at those institutions. The Partnering Resources In Ministry Education roster, from which the book takes its name, is comprised of a dozen nationally and internationally distinguished educational and research training centers in a variety of fields to which our student-clients go in order to fulfill their educational venue components. Next only to the SICC relationships, these constitute the backbone of the Foundation's collaborative cooperation with other independent institutions. Not at any point does the Foundation attempt to dictate matters affecting these institutions' own certification requirements. Rather, we expect and insist that the PRIME institutions maintain their very own self-understood requirements to which Foundation students must subscribe if they are to receive those institutions' certificates of completion. Upon receipt of the completion certificates and with the endorsement of the directors of those institutional programs, our student-clients can then receive the Foundation's graduate degrees for work completed there.

(C) Recognized and Endorsed institutions, of which there are over forty at the writing of this book, consist of educational, training, and research study centers here and abroad with which the Foundation has established formal relationships. In an exchange of correspondence, both institutions have entered into a

76

reciprocating acknowledgment such that when Foundation students come to these R & E institutions to secure a Unit of Study in the form of a course, seminar, workshop, or conference, this reciprocal acknowledgment works to the advantage of the student. Over the years, these institutions, as with PRIME institutions, have found that their enrollment benefits from the fact that the Foundation annually has over three hundred graduate students attending educational venues sponsored by R & E institutions.

(D) Approved Venue Sites Roster. Prior to the Foundation approaching an educational institution for the creation of an R & E relationship, we have historically tested the effectiveness of various institutional offerings, particularly as evaluated by our students who have participated in these educational venues. Our students are not required to take their Units of Study at either the PRIME or the R & E institutions, rather, these relationships have been cultivated for the ease of access by our students. However, they are at liberty to pursue other institutions and educational venues which they themselves have identified. When such experiences prove helpful to the student as assessed and evaluated by the student, we then place those institutions on a roster entitled, Approved Venue Sites. In terms of collaboration, these AVS institutions are at the initial level of recognition. When they do fulfill a perceived need as determined by our students and faculty, then the Foundation approaches them for a possible Recognized and Endorsed Relationship.

(E) Consultative Ecclesial Bodies. For a good number of years, the Foundation has maintained consultative relationships with a number of religious denominations and ecclesiastical judicatories both in the U.S. and throughout the world. By designating an official *liaison officer* from their own professional staff, these international bodies provide the Foundation with much valuable insight into the direction that ministry education is going and needs to go as we address the future and the ongoing training of professionals in all cognates of ministry.

Now that I have explained somewhat the nature and scope of these multi-leveled relationships maintained by the Foundation, a quick recitation of our degree programs and a profile of our students might be in order. The Foundation offers graduate degrees at the master's and doctoral level in both professional and academic fields of study. The development of various degree programs is directly linked to the affiliations we establish and maintain in these relevant fields. All degree programs are in some cognate of ministry as explained and identified above. All students are in some form of ministry and are referred to, therefore, as "ministry professionals," which means that they are in a human service field of professional work. Our master's degrees all require an undergraduate degree and five years' experience in the relevant field of ministry. Our professional doctorates require a bachelor's and master's degree and five years professional experience as a minimum requirement. Our academic doctorates require a bachelor's, master's, and professional doctorate and five years experience in order to be considered for acceptance. Over 80% of our students hold ordination or clergy status within a faith tradition and 85% of our professional doctoral students hold a second master's degree in a cognate field of ministry upon entry. The average age of our students is 49 years with over twenty years of professional experience in their chosen fields of ministry.

With this level of academic and professional training and experience upon entry into the Foundation's degree programs, the expectations placed upon the student are high and the performance level is equally so. The intent is to set the bar extremely high for entry so that the implementation of the new paradigm of collaboration and consultation between student as client and faculty/administration as colleagues can be maximized to its greatest advantage. Since all of our professional veterans already have at least two, and in many instances three or more, graduate degrees from traditionalist institutions, they are fully cognizant of the preset curriculum approach to education and, therefore, of the absolute difference in educational philosophy embodied by the Foundation. Students come to the Foundation on the basis of a referral from a graduate of a Foundation degree program at a rate of 95%. Since most professionals have happily gone through the hoop-jumping form of graduate education in the past, our professional clients are now looking for more control, more say in their education, more management of their own learning opportunities and advancement. They come to us as clients and we deal with them as collaborative consultants and colleagues in the diverse fields of ministry education.

Students choose the topic.

The Foundation is structurally and philosophically committed to the New Paradigm of collaborative education. This new paradigm is built upon a collegial relationship between professional students as clients and the Foundation, and between the Foundation and other educational venue providing institutions. We function as host and home to the professional desiring to develop a personalized educational portfolio in the pursuit of a graduate or terminal degree.

Through a self-selective process, professional veterans come to the Foundation instead of some other educational venue owing to the uniqueness of our program design. For those who are seeking a standardized degree program, we discourage their consideration of the Foundation since we know that particular type of student will be lost and disappointed. It takes a particular kind of professional to feel comfortable in this sort of consultative environment, one willing to assert ownership over the degree planning process, initiate inquiries into various educational opportunities for study, etc. When a professional comes to us, they have chosen us precisely because of our model, not in spite of it. If the inquiring professional asks standardization-type questions regarding our degree programs, we immediately begin to point them in the direction of just the right educational venue of which we are aware, thereby fulfilling a sort of referral service to other graduate programs for the inquiring prospective student. However, when a professional is finally admitted into our program – granted, the admissions bar is set rather high – confidence is likewise high that he/she will be quite successful in completing the program. Our high percentage of degree completion seems to validate this process.

Upon acceptance into a specific degree program, all Foundation students must come to Indiana for a one-day Orientation Session. This is a requirement whether the student is coming from Chicago or Hong Kong, Cairo or St. Louis. They must come to the Foundation and spend the day with the administrative staff in an orientation designed to fully acquaint them with both the collaborative philosophy of the institution as well as with the plethora of educational venues from which they might choose to select a learning experience. They are oriented to our various and sundry affiliations, associations, consultative relationships, etc. And, finally, and most importantly, the senior staff sit with the new student to assist in the initial development of what often proves to be a preliminary plan of study, the educational portfolio.

This portfolio will, naturally, go through a series of changes and evolving developments, all under the direction of the student and the nurturing oversight of the administration and faculty. These changes occur in direct relationship to the student's broadening perspective and widening horizons gleaned from the educational experiences being accrued in the degree process. Gradually and finally, the portfolio comes to a level of operative fruition towards the end of the process of accumulating educational Units of Study. At this point, the project is taken in hand. Of that, more later. But in this process of portfolio development, the student-client takes the lead and exercises jurisdiction over the content components of the personalized degree program.

The Foundation has established required components for each of our degree programs called Units of Study. The content for these required units, however, is not determined by the Foundation but by the student. So if a student wishes to fulfill one Unit of Study by doing something in clinical pastoral education or liturgical studies or the history of Jewish thought in 19th century Poland, we can arrange it. Sometimes the professional student wishes to radically diversify the educational components of the degree program – doing a unit in liturgy, scripture, counseling, and administration, while others wish to concentrate all of their required Units of Study in one particular field of professional practice, say in counseling, with Units of Study in clinical assessment, family systems, psychoanalytic modalities of therapy, and maybe an advanced seminar in logotherapy.

The student "fills the Units of Study" with the contents relevant to his/her own professional interest and field of practice. Often, students come to accelerate or embellish their already existing specialization while others come to "change ladders," maybe moving from parish ministry to institutional chaplaincy. Whatever the incentive to take a terminal degree, the student exercises jurisdiction over his/her own educational destiny. The faculty and administration are actively engaged in identifying and establishing relationships with worthy educational venues; the student is actively engaged in identifying and pursuing educational experiences relevant to his/her degree program and professional aspirations or needs. This is where the collaborative consultation comes into play for both the professional veteran and the Foundation.

Students choose the time.

In addition to being free, in the selecting of the topics for the required Units of Study for any particular degree program, the student-client is also completely in charge of selecting the time of study. This, of course, has been one of the major deterrents for many professionals seeking the terminal degree, viz., not being able to take off the time required by the traditionalist institution to do the required courses. Not so with the New Paradigm of collaborative education. The student determines the timetable, not the faculty or the institution.

Naturally, this calls for the hosting institution of these seasoned veterans to be responsive to the professional demands of the workplace rather than the faculty-generated demands of the academy. It all comes down to a question of who is serving whom

– is the institution at the service of the student-client, or vice versa? In the case of the latter, we have the traditionalist institution setting the curriculum and determining the times when the required educational experiences can be accessed by the student.

In the case of the former, we have the hosting institution deferring to the workplace demands placed upon the student-client such that educational venues are designed and presented at the convenience of the consumer. With undergraduates, such a highhanded posture as seen in the traditionalist institution might still be gotten away with though one wonders today. However, with the level of competition in the academy for the consumer, we might question whether or not that sort of unilateral educational provider can last indefinitely. With seasoned professionals, who most, if not all, are already well placed and are now looking to elevate their credentials to the highest rung on the ladder, highhandedness will never do.

Early on the Foundation made a commitment to put in place an educational methodology which addressed and responded to the need for time-flexibility. We knew our students were consistently well placed in the workplace and, therefore, would not be the least inclined to give up their professional employment for the pursuit and securing of a terminal degree. If the degree were to be pursued for the purpose of topping off their formal education, it would necessarily have to be within the context of maintaining fulltime employment. We have found, contrary to traditionalist institutions' misplaced fears that employment would be a deterrent to quality performance, that the very fact that all of our incoming students hold professional positions takes them to a higher level of performance than the student who only has to attend class and write papers.

Thus, we have created a radically flexible degree program such that our students are in sole control of when they attend courses, workshops, conferences, seminars, all for the purpose of accumulating Units of Study at their own selected educational

82

venues. Here again we see the interaction of "topic, place, and time" and the student, not the faculty or institution, controls all three variables.

Students choose the place.

At the Foundation, in addition to encouraging the student-client to set the topics to be pursued in the educational portfolio, we also encourage that same professional to take advantage of a veritable educational smorgasbord out there in the wide world. Why take all of one's studies from one place, one faculty, on one campus, with only one library? Why not reach out and venture into new and creatively dynamic places of learning, institutes, research centers, training seminars offered through the various national professional organizations, etc.? We have students who, when putting together their portfolio, seek to spread the required Units of Study around to a variety of venues – say, taking one unit at the Jung Institute in Zurich, another at the Mayo Clinic, and yet another at Princeton's Center for Continuing Education, maybe finishing up with a Unit of Study at Oxford University or the Centro Pro Unione in Rome with the Franciscan Friars of the Atonement. Why not? We can arrange it.

If the new paradigm institution is committed to presenting seasoned veteran students with the opportunity to maximize their learning opportunities, then this sort of variety in educational venues is the way to go. These educational venues, as noted earlier, function at four levels of relationship with the Foundation and our students, though not limited to these affiliated institutions, and therefore, have easy and ready access to some of the leading educational venues in this country and abroad.

From the four-tiered level of inter-institutional associations and relationships cited above, it is clear that the Foundation has put in place a very convenient mechanism for the wide-ranging opportunity of educational venue selection. Our students are not limited to our faculty, our library, our curriculum, or our timetable. Rather, they set the topic, they identify the place, the time, and, finally, and very importantly, they determine the cost of their overall degree program.

Students control the cost.

Today, it is almost criminal what students have to pay to earn a terminal degree in the field of ministry. I have recently published a book indirectly addressing this issue. The book focused upon the widespread phenomenon of All-But-Dissertation (ABD) students in the field of theology and its cognates in religious studies. The book, entitled, *UNFINISHED BUSINESS: The Terminal All-But-Dissertation Phenomenon in American Higher Education (A National Study of Failures to Complete Doctoral Studies in Theology,* Cloverdale Books, 2003*)* explores the great contrast in the failure to complete doctoral studies in theology and religious studies between the European community, particularly England and Germany, where the ABD phenomenon hardly exists at all, and the U.S., where the failure rate is in double digits. And, what's more, there seems to be a direct correlation in the data between the high cost of tuition and the failure rate such that the higher the cost, the higher the failure rate!

The findings, based on data generated from a study of the top twenty doctoral degree granting institutions in the U.S., suggest that there is a "systemic problem" within the institutions themselves. That is to say, there seems to be a real lag in the ongoing support of the doctoral student once he/she has completed the residency, taken the qualifying exams, and finished the language requirements. Not only is the actual writing of the dissertation in itself a rather lonely business, but the institution and its faculty decidedly lose interest in the doctoral student at this level, preferring rather to place its attention, nurture, and care upon the new incoming beginning doctoral student and, thus, diverting its attention from the older, almost, but not quite done, student.

There is, unfortunately, a rather disturbing suggestion in the data that this redirecting of administrative and faculty attention is not unrelated to the difference in the level of fees being paid. There is, we might point out, a wide disparity between the older student writing a dissertation and, thus, not paying tuition, but rather a mere maintenance fee and the new incoming doctoral student who is paying full price for the experience. A second and equally disturbing finding suggests that there is a direct and irrefutable correlation between the failure rate and the type of faculty assigned to doctoral students as thesis supervisors, with the more outstanding faculty having a high success rate of completion and the less respected, less published, less profiled faculty having a miserably low rate of completion. This reality as well as its inevitability, too, seems to be quite clearly known by the faculty when supervisors are being appointed.

But, that was another book. When it comes to the Foundation, we are extremely keen to see to it that our doctoral students avoid any borrowing of money for the securing of the degree. We prefer a pay-as-you-go plan of attack on the tuition costs and we also maintain an in-house payment plan that does not assess interest on tuition costs, yet the student must complete the payments prior to graduation. By allowing the student to determine where, when, and what he/she studies, the Foundation concomitantly empowers the student to profoundly control costs. Though a student may "wish I had" studied in Oxford or Rome or the Mayo, the student's choice of venue determines the price the degree will eventually cost.

We might, however, point out here that due to our use of a variety of educational venue options, our students do, at a rather high percentage, attend Oxford and Rome as well as the Mayo Foundation and the Jung Institute in Zurich. They may take just a single Unit of Study there, but it nevertheless shows up on the transcript as one of their venues of study. Among professionals practicing in the field, bragging rights are not to be discounted out of hand.

The Foundation charges an administrative fee for the hosting of the student and the management of the student's collaboratively developed educational portfolio. By casting the portfolio in an evolving mode, students can, following each Unit of Study, determine the next level of costs as they select the next venue for a Unit of Study. The total cost of a degree consists of the Foundation's administrative fee plus the costs of each of the venues of study accumulated in the process of completing the degree. Rather than encourage government or personal loans, the Foundation carries the loan itself without interest with the stipulation that all fees are paid prior to graduation.

Foundation tuition runs between $4,500.00 and $6,500.00, depending on whether it is a master's degree or doctoral degree being pursued and whether it is a professional or an academic degree. We find that students are often astounded at our low costs. However, on top of Foundation fees, the student must pay the educational venue fees. For example, the total cost of our Doctor of Ministry will run at $3,000.00 to Oxford University plus $5,500.00 to the Foundation. These costs can go up or down, depending on the other venue selections, say, if a Ph.D. in Pastoral Psychology decides to do all of the educational venues at a state university graduate school across town from where he/she lives, thus making the cost unbelievably low, or prefers to do a combination of venues at UC/Berkeley, Harvard, the Mayo, and Zurich, making the cost considerably higher.

Of course, the Foundation is fully aware that we as a New Paradigm institution have intentionally avoided some of the major operating costs of traditionalist institutions. We have never said that our way was the only way; rather, we have always said that our way is an alternative but equally viable way of offering professional and doctoral level training to seasoned veteran professionals seeking to advance themselves in their careers. For example, we have no campus grounds to maintain as our office building in downtown South Bend, Indiana, sits immediately beside a small carefully maintained city park, thus providing a place for our visiting students to sit under the maple trees and enjoy the courthouse lawn upon which our building sits. By saving the cost of grounds maintenance, we save considerably in operating costs. Furthermore, we have a long-term lease on a beautiful suite in The Tower Building, a landmark on the National Register as an Historic Building. Our neo-gothic windows overlook the Old Courthouse and its splendid grounds which host a rather grand Civil War Monument to Indiana's Union soldiers who served and died in battle.

Avoiding building and grounds maintenance goes a long way in keeping student fees under control. Furthermore, we have no refectory for our students, though we provide coffee and tea in-house during the Orientation Session. Rather, we have nine restaurants and cafes within three city blocks of The Tower Building, which itself is twelve stories high and towers in its gargoyle splendor over the very heart of the city. Our students come to us for the Orientation Session and, when desired, return for a personal consultation which is not required but always available, and then they return finally to graduate. Immediately across the street from the Foundation is the City Center's Holiday Inn with which we have a corporate pricing arrangement to the great financial benefit of our students, and two blocks down is the Marriott Inn which is attached to the Century Civic Center and Plaza, where we host our annual gala Convocations and Graduation ceremonies.

No campus, no grounds, no refectory, all go towards low fees. Since we prefer to provide an internet library (more later on this key point), the buying of books and paying of library staff does not exist either! For a bookstore, we use Amazon.com primarily, but since we have both Barnes & Noble and Borders in town, students wishing to buy books are directed to these privately maintained businesses for that purpose. Thanks to Jostens, students are provided rings, robes, etc., with no added surcharge from the Foundation.

Finally, when it comes to faculty, we have opted for the New Paradigm model of a contract faculty, thus avoiding either tenure or long-term faculty who are paid based on years of service rather than services rendered. Certainly, the old paradigm and traditionalist institutions cannot function in this fashion and we fully applaud their ongoing commitment to the old paradigm. Indeed, many of the old paradigm institutions constitute our most popular and effective educational venues and we send hundreds of students to them annually to take their courses and to pay their fees. But the Foundation itself does not maintain a permanently staffed faculty other than our senior administrators who also hold named professorships in their respective fields. However, our contract faculty is second to none in international reputation and published scholarship. One needs only to peruse our faculty roster for both Foundation Faculty and Tutorial Faculty to see the depth of scholarship and reputation evidenced at the Foundation.

Our faculty engage in four levels of function for the Foundation, and these we have discussed in some detail earlier in this book. These functions include (1) involvement with the administration in the planning and development of new degree programs, (2) the evaluation and assessment of the written work of our students required of each educational venue, (3) the supervision of theses and dissertations, and (4) the offering, upon demand, of private tutorials in their own personal fields of expertise.

In the interest of fostering creativity on the part of our veteran students in the pursuit of their own educational goals while securing their terminal degree, and in demonstration of the Foundation's genuine commitment to collaborative education in working with students and institutions, the Foundation has put in place a system of Tutorials and Independent Study options and opportunities. Each is designed to capitalize on the initiative of the veteran professional student who, more often than not, has a much better idea of what is needed than a faculty advisor. Indeed, often the advising is in reverse, namely, this type and quality of student is often involved in the advising of the faculty as to what needs to be made available in relationship to what is most desired.

The Tutorial program at the Foundation is built around the model of tutoring employed at Oxford University, albeit an intensified version. This model, which is hundreds of years old, has brought great distinction to that august institution and the Foundation has found that our veteran students greatly admire its strengths. The system profoundly enhances student initiative and greatly focuses the study of the student and the consultative relationship with the faculty involved. The Foundation has an ongoing contractual relationship with a large number of distinguished national and international scholars who hold teaching posts at the best institutions both here and abroad. These contracts are between the Foundation and the scholar, and students are made aware of both the roster of Tutorial Faculty and Topics and also are encouraged to identify scholars not on the Roster with whom they very much wish to study. In such instances, those particularly selected scholars are approached by the student as to whether a tutorial might be in the offing and, if so, the Foundation then contracts with that scholar to function as a Tutor. If scholars so desire, they may be added to the Tutorial Roster for further tutorials as interest and occasion arise.

The Tutorial is set up rather simply. Once contacts and contracts have been settled, the student having mutually agreed with the Tutor as to actual topic and required readings, the student goes to the Tutor (where ever in the world that tutor may hold a teaching post) and for five days meets one hour for a discussion of the pre-assigned readings set for each of the five one-hour daily sessions. The student is required to bring to each session, commencing with the first one, a three to five page reflective paper on the pre-assigned readings. This paper, read out by the student within the context of the tutorial, constitutes the basis for the daily one-hour discussion. As the student reads out the paper, the tutor questions, probes, inquires, suggests, challenges, etc., the student on the basis of the written document which has been produced for that day.

At the end of the five one-hour daily tutorial sessions, the Tutor's obligation is fulfilled and the Foundation sends the contracted fee. The student, on the other hand, takes the accumulated 15 - 25 pages of draft work and condenses them into a coherent 12 - 15 page scholarly paper which is submitted to the Foundation's faculty, not the Tutor. In the Oxford tradition of radical separation of tutoring and examining (tutors teach and examiners examine and they are never the same person for the same student!), the Tutor is out of the evaluation loop. The Foundation's own faculty, at this point, become directly engaged in the evaluation process and, in due course, the student is apprised of the score earned for the written paper required of the tutorial.

The Independent Study works differently. For the enterprising veteran student, the opportunity exists for the suggesting of a topic of research and study interest of special value and concern to the student. If a student wishes to propose a topic of research and writing, the proposal is made in terms of both a topic with descriptive paragraph explaining the parameters of the topic and the value of the topic to the concerned student along with a well developed resource bibliography to be used in the writing of a major scholarly paper of 12 - 15 pages. Once the Independent Study topic has been approved by the relevant faculty, the student has six months to complete the research and writing of the project, submitting the finished paper directly to the faculty of the Foundation. The paper is duly evaluated and the student receives the credit.

By offering both the Tutorial and the Independent Study, the Foundation has extended the collaborative educational model of the New Paradigm to its fullest extent, relying heavily both upon the initiative of the independent-minded veteran student and the collaboration with Tutorial Faculty in the process. In both instances, the student stands to benefit immensely owing to both the flexibility of the subject matter and the personal initiative called for in this process of student-driven education.

Another feature of the Foundation's cost-controlling philosophy in the new paradigm is that of offering scholarships, fellowships, and prizes. Our three Fellowships constitute the highest level of academic achievement recognized by the Foundation Faculty. The three are the John Macquarrie Fellowship in Philosophical

Theology, named in honor of our most distinguished faculty member and funded from the generosity of Canon Macquarrie's autobiography; the Imam Malik Fellowship in Islamic Studies; and the Rabbi Abraham Joshua Heschel Fellowship in Jewish Studies. These fellowships are prestigious by Foundation standards and eagerly sought and deeply admired by our students and alumni/ae. Yet, they constitute a cash prize awarded at Graduation worth only about 10% of the tuition fees of the Foundation. There are a plethora of scholarships, each carrying a name designating some outstanding person in the field of human service – Thurgood Marshall, César Chávez, Katie Ferguson, Rabbi Isaac Wise, Rabi'a al'-Adawiyya, Horace Bushnell, President Jimmy Carter, etc. These scholarships constitute about 10% of the student fees for the desired degree as well and are, likewise, awarded at the time of the beginning of a degree program and paid towards the last half of the students' fees to the Foundation. The prizes constitute about 20% of a graduating student's fees towards the next advanced degree taken at the Foundation and are named in particular fields of ministry and service including parish ministry, pastoral care and counseling, Islamic and Jewish history, the creative arts, and sacred music. All of these things – no campus, no grounds, no buildings, no refectory, no library, no bookstore, contract faculty, modest scholarships/fellowships/prizes – all conspire to control costs. Then, by empowering the student to select educational venues affordable and practical to the student's professional interest, what emerges is an achievable degree without financial ruin or indebtedness as a major characteristic of the experience.

The Venues

We like what they do.

A fundamental feature of the New Paradigm of which the Foundation proudly imagines itself being a leading exemplar is that of the concept of educational venue providers serving our students as a collaborative effort in professional education. The concept of networking already existing and gradually producing new forms of learning experiences into a collegial collaboration resulting in a student-tailored doctoral degree program is an original act of creativity. We are aware of that and do not cower from the criticism which might come from traditionalist institutions; institutions, I might add, all of which are beneficiaries of the Foundation as we send hundreds of fee-paying students to their campuses annually.

The Foundation's task, shared by faculty and administration, is the identification and evaluation of these existing and emerging educational venues. Assessing their merits for the benefit of our student-clients seeking a range of innovative and traditionalist educational opportunities is a major function of the Foundation. Instead of one faculty, one curriculum, one campus, one library, and one coffee shop, we offer them the world and all that's in it! We find the programs and offer them to our students. Offer is the operative word here, and not require, as we are committed to acknowledging and honoring the treasury of experience these seasoned veterans bring to their doctoral studies. They choose, they design, they decide, they consult, they act – the Foundation is here to assist them in that process.

We go everywhere, look at everything, consider every possibility, evaluate every legitimate offering of education. And our rosters of PRIME, R & E, and AVS affiliations reflect that range and that diversity. Furthermore, the Foundation is not merely limited to the offerings of the traditionalist graduate schools, though most of our students take some of their Units of Study at such places. We embrace these relationships and encourage our students to pursue such opportunities as Harvard, Yale, and Princeton have to offer. Yet, we also encourage adventurous venues which stretch the mold and offer new and fresh perspectives on all dimensions of professional practice. So we have relationships not only with the major university centers of North America and Europe, but we also have established various levels of affiliation with training institutes, research centers, and educational associations, ranging from the Mayo Foundation and the Cape Code Institute to the

Jung Institute in Zurich and the Tao Fong Shan Retreat Center in Hong Kong. If students want to study Native American spirituality, we get them off to the Vancouver School of Theology, or if they want to study the enneagram or family systems off they go to the Hiebert Institute or the Chicago Family Center, and the list goes on for dozens and dozens of internationally respected educational venues. And, if a student identifies an educational venue which has not yet established a relationship with the Foundation, that student is welcome to present descriptive materials for approval of this new site. We in turn, once the assessment is complete, initiate contact and set about establishing one level of relationship or another. The whole idea is NOT to go it alone but to see collaboration in the professional training of seasoned practitioners.

Many eggs, one basket!

The purpose of the educational portfolio then, of course, is to keep all of the student's eggs in a manageable basket – a plethora of educational experiences and learning venues all leading to the earning of the graduate or doctoral degree under the nurture and consultative care of the Foundation's faculty and administration. While some professionals come to us specifically with the intention of doing all of their work at Oxford University or at the Centro Pro Unione in Rome, others come in hopes of spreading their Units of Study around the country or around the globe.

Not uncommon is the professional practitioner in counseling or psychotherapy who comes with an eye towards a unit in Zurich with the Jungians, another at the Mayo Clinic, while yet another at a mediation training program in New York or Houston. Commonly, these clients will throw in a private tutorial with a scholar specifically in their field of dissertation research as I saw recently with an Imam student whose specialty and dissertation was the history of Bosnian Muslims in America. So he got himself off to the Faculty of Islamic Studies in Sarajevo for a private tutorial with their leading historian!

93

The comfort level runs high for our students who know that their educational portfolio has been developed with their own personal oversight and initiative and can at any point be altered or modified to suit their changing needs and interests. The Foundation's faculty and administration is here to assure those student-clients of their progress, report on work completed, and monitor work yet to be done, and, most importantly, continually facilitate the completion of Units of Study and the thesis or dissertation under careful supervision by the faculty. Since we require the most outstanding scholars in the relevant fields of research being done for dissertations to serve as faculty supervisors, our confidence is always high when a dissertation comes in with the endorsement of the Ordinarius as a completed work of scholarship worthy of a Doctor of Philosophy or Doctor of Theology designation.

Their certificate, our degree!

Another important feature of the Foundation's commitment to collaborative professional education is the acknowledgment of the value of work done elsewhere which does not lead to a degree at all but perhaps a certification or endorsement or some other identifiable credential based upon an educational experience. These learning venues exist all over the country and elsewhere, (research and study institutes, training programs of all kinds), which offer intensive short-term programs of professional learning but, in themselves, do not lead to a degree.

The Foundation is keen to cluster these types of certifications and assess their academic merits and reward the student accordingly. If one goes to the Harvard Leadership Institute or a major seminar at the Princeton Center for Continuing Education, they receive a documented credential, certificate of completion, or some such thing, but the Foundation, in turn, based upon careful evaluation, offers degree credit leading to the desired program. If a particular educational program is granted meritorious assessment by Harvard or Princeton, the Foundation is prepared to extend that assessment to doctoral credit. The same is true for many institutions in all kinds of fields. We are prepared to gather variously related certificates of completion and count those toward the completion of our doctoral requirements.

For instance, with PRIME institutions such as the Alamance Regional Medical Center in North Carolina or Alexian Brothers Medical Center in Chicago, a student can complete their training program in Clinical Pastoral Education and present their documentation to the Foundation along with a written exit project and receive complete credit towards our Doctor of Ministry degree. Why should a student have to repeat the same kind of training with us for our degree if they have already done the training elsewhere? There is little sense or fairness in requiring the repeating or extending of work merely to fulfill some preset requirements for an institution's degree program.

If the student has done the work and it has not been credited towards another degree, we give them credit toward their degree with us. Our only involvement is making sure of the quality of the educational venue and the merits of the certification earned. So where a major training center may be empowered to award a distinguished certificate of completion, the Foundation will award a degree. If one takes their residency at Oxford University or the Centro Pro Unione in Rome and receives the completion certificate, the Foundation will honor that certificate by giving academic credit for it to the benefit of the student seeking our terminal degree. If it is good enough for Oxford and Rome, Harvard and Princeton, it is good enough for the Foundation, and we validate the learning by awarding the degree.

Mr. Certificate, Dr. Degree.

In an earlier time in this country, the terminal degree was not so common and certainly not expected of those in professional ministry. In medicine, unlike the British practice of awarding a bachelor's degree for the actual practice of medicine, the American system followed the Europeans and at Johns Hopkins Medical School and other early medical colleges the practice began immediately to award a doctor's degree for the first professional practitioner's credential. And not until the mid-1900s did we see law schools move away from the traditional L.L.B., Bachelor of Laws, to the now first practitioner's degree of Juris Doctor (J.D.). Divinity schools were much more cautious, conservative if you will, in imagining a clergy person's practicing with a professional terminal degree. The origin of this Doctor of Ministry is fascinating and few can tell it with more animation and enthusiasm than Krister Stendahl of Harvard University.

However, what once was the practitioner's degree for ministry at Oxford and Cambridge, the B.A. degree, when brought to this country soon became a post-bachelor's degree called a Bachelor of Divinity which was, in reality, a three-year graduate degree built upon a four year undergraduate degree. Even when I went off to seminary, the expectation was that clergy students would pursue the B.D. first, a three-year course of graduate study with a solid Bachelor of Arts as the foundation. This was expected of those intending to enter parish ministry. Being a member of the Society of Friends (we have no clergy in our tradition), I proceeded to take the M.A. and Ph.D., having earned my B.A. already. This two-option sequence, either the B.A., M.A., Ph.D. for intended teaching career, or the B.A., B.D., and possibly M.Th. for parish ministry, was most common.

Then, in the mid-1960s, the theological community stepped forward with the notion that the B.D. did not reflect in the nomenclature the level of training required and gained by that degree, so we saw the evolution of the Master of Divinity, still not a terminal doctor's degree as with law and medicine, yet a step forward with the credentialing titles. At about the same time, the theological community began to explore, under the leadership of Dean Stendahl of Harvard and others, the creation of a *bona fide* terminal doctor's degree for parish clergy with a particular emphasis upon pastoral praxis rather than academic research and scholarship. It eventually came into being, with a substantial amount of fascinating birth pains, as the Doctor of Ministry. Most seminaries had no idea how to deal with a terminal professional doctor's degree, so for several years and at most seminaries, the

D.Min. was merely thought of as a "little Ph.D." and nothing more.

It was sad to see the struggling traditionalist institutions and academic faculties trying to put together a professional doctorate, given their traditional commitments to research-based scholarship. It was some time before there came the realization that there is a legitimate place for a genuinely "professional" doctor's degree based upon praxis-oriented curricula rather than academic curricula, and that the professional doctorate had just as much integrity and pride of place as the academic doctorate. Even today, some seminaries and divinity schools have failed miserably in identifying and validating the difference. The result of this failure, sad to say, has been many disappointed and disillusioned ministry professionals commencing and ceasing their doctoral studies. The Foundation, I am pleased to say, gets a disproportionately large number of this type of student enrolling in our degree programs.

Of course, 2005 is not 1955, and the professional demands and expectations are much different and more specific today in ministry than they were fifty years ago. Not only that, but we see the rabbinate in Judaism and the imams of the Muslim community being forced, inevitably, to continue to redefine the nature of their work and leadership in response to growing expectations from both the Jewish and Muslim communities, based upon their perception of the role of the religious leader in modern day society.

The demand for a terminal degree in ministry has almost become standard practice in the mainline denominations of America and, not surprisingly, one begins to sense the same thing occurring in the United Kingdom. To be "Dr. Degree" rather than merely "Mr. Certificate" in the practicing professions of ministry, counseling, mediation, teaching, administration, health care, etc., is to be placed into an entirely different category of treatment by the public and of respect within the professional ranks of one's colleagues.

97

If we try to pretend that this credentialing mania does not exist, we demonstrate our own naïveté. To attempt to opt out of the degree-seeking credentialing mania is to assure one's own lack of success in the field of practice. Hardly a field of professional practice exists today in this country which does not expect that the doctor's degree will be the final rung on the ladder of training and expertise. Without it, one is still just a lay person whether he/she likes it or not. I have begun to notice that even the pharmacists of Wal-Mart have earned their doctorates, called a Pharm.D. The trend cannot be reversed, even if we end up with a large number of professionals educated beyond their intelligence.

And since there are so many traditionalist institutions which have simply tried to put together doctoral degree programs based upon the rules and regulations of the undergraduate curriculum or the graduate degree designed early on as the first degree of professional practice, the Foundation has rather determined to embrace the New Paradigm, to present a radical philosophy of collaborative education which empowers the seasoned veteran student as client with jurisdiction rights over the development and execution of doctoral studies designed to address his/her specific and personal needs and ambitions.

How many certificates make a degree?

The intent from the beginning of the Foundation's involvement in this form of collaborative education, the creation of the New Paradigm, if you will, was to empower those who were already seasoned practitioners in the various cognate fields of ministry. We set out to do this by acknowledging and validating their wide range of educational experiences which would then result in the earning of a terminal degree. That intention and that focus has not wavered over the twenty-two years of my administration. Early on we saw clergy, laity, and members of religious orders coming through our doors with a packet of distinguished certifications and documented evidence of upper-level professional training from distinguished and internationally respected research, study, and training institutes. And yet, even with multiple master's, multiple certifications, diplomate status within professional organizations, there was no sign of a doctor's degree.

When we measured these packets of training against the normative standards for doctoral degrees, we found these professionals to not only be NOT lacking in terms of both formalized educational experience and credentialed and certified training, but more often than not well over the top. The Foundation simply set about creating an environment, a consultative and collaborative environment, within which these professionals could realize their aspirations of completing a doctor's degree within the confines of their own professional working parameters. And to our great satisfaction, but not surprise, we found that many of these national and international training, research, and study centers were pleased to have the Foundation validate their certificates with our degrees. In fact, in some instances, the Foundation has become the credit-awarding institution for certificate-level training at some international institutes.

The Projects

Getting the job done.

The work of the student and the work of the Foundation are not complete until the presenting of the dissertation for oral defense before our faculty, or, in the case of professional doctorates rather than academic ones, the presentation of a completed project. The Foundation has always made a radical distinction between academic degrees and professional degrees, not in terms of quality of work or level of work, but in terms of type of work. As noted earlier, we came on the scene right when the theological community was attempting to define a professional doctorate in such a fashion as to not disparage the academic doctorates common in the academy and yet do justice to the difference.

The professional degrees at the Foundation, both master's and doctorates, are built around a series of accumulated Units of Study from the student's own selections as developed in the educational portfolio. The counterbalance component of any professional degree is the exit project, not necessarily a thesis. The balance comes into play when the student integrates both the educational experiences gained from the variety of venues selected with the experience he/she has brought to the learning adventure. All of this educated training is focused upon a "praxis" project addressing an issue, a problem, and task at hand, a proposal to be made, a plan to be implemented. The least valuable experience of all at this level of study and learning is an exit project that is merely perceived as the last hurdle over which a student must leap in order to complete the degree program.

On the contrary, the exit projects of our professional degrees are thought of as reflecting the last and best effort in the learning process and must be developed to do just that. Therefore, it is to the student, rather than a preset agenda of some faculty member, that the Foundation looks for the selection of the topic and execution of the project. This project must be a first and last love of the student, an effort demanding the expenditure of such energy that only a genuine passion for the subject can see it through to fruition. Many of our professional degree projects get published, not just by diocesan presses but by some of the leading houses in the country. This is because we encourage our professional students to imagine "making a contribution" to their particular field of ministry. If the project is truly meaningful and valuable to themselves in their own specialized field of work, then it might just prove of value to others in like situations of service.

The project is written in collaboration with a student-selected Project Consultant. This person is a professional in the field with the same degree being sought by our student. The relationship is non-stipendiary and, thus, constitutes a collegial favor. Many of our 1,500 alumni/ae volunteer regularly to serve in this capacity, and we have within our alumni/ae specialists in every conceivable branch of human service ministries. The relationship between students and the Foundation's administration and faculty is one of collaborative consultation, a relationship such that students merely inform the Foundation what they are pursuing as an exit project rather than the other way around. We have set the bar high for professionals to enter our program; we likewise set the bar high for professional pride, expectation, and accomplishment. These students are self-challenged to put forth their very best effort on the exit project rather than attempting merely to "skim through." And the Project Consultant serves as a professional reminder at every stage of development in the execution of this project.

Often the selection of a Project Consultant constitutes a major event in the student-client career as the Project Consultant can and does often prove of real benefit professionally. As the student is to work closely with the Project Consultant in the development of the topic and the bringing of it to fruition, the relationship between student and Project Consultant can be extremely meaningful. Students are encouraged to select a Project Consultant who is in the arena of professional work in which the student aspires to be situated.

There are many stories I have collected over the years of students who have benefited professionally for just the right selection of a Project Consultant. Two come immediately to mind. First, a young priest working in a parish in the suburbs of Dublin wanted very much to work inside the Holy Office at the Vatican. As he knew no one in that post, I suggested he ask his bishop if he knew someone. Sure enough, the bishop had a friend inside the Holy Office who agreed to serve as Project Consultant to the young Irish priest. When the project was completed, we received a splendid letter of endorsement from the Holy Office on Vatican stationery and six months later another letter on the same stationery from our young Irish priest who had, as a matter of fact, gotten the call to the Vatican based on the quality of his project and the endorsement of his Project Consultant.

Another such instance comes to mind. A young student working on her D.Min. in spiritual direction was serving as adjunct to a local seminary where she very much aspired to become a fulltime faculty member on a tenure-track appointment, but was continually retained as adjunct while working for a retreat center fulltime. She decided to ask the Dean of the seminary to serve as her Project Consultant and after completing the project and receiving her degree, the Dean offered her a tenure-track appointment where she now holds tenure and teaches fulltime. Foundation students are encouraged to be Machiavellian in the pursuit of their professional goals within the context of completing their degree requirements.

When the professional project is completed and the Project Consultant has signed off on evaluation papers (not that the Project Consultant has jurisdiction over pass/fail of the student but the desire of our faculty is to have an outside evaluation nevertheless), a copy is sent to the Foundation for distribution to the relevant colleagues within the ranks of the professional faculty. Once the project has been examined for standards of performance, completeness of treatment, and quality of presentation (we keep this time frame to within two weeks as our faculty are extremely busy during the early months of the year), the student is notified by the Foundation of their completion status.

If the project is received by February 1st and receives Foundation acceptance and approval, the student graduates the first Friday of May. This is a standing rule. If the project is not accepted, the student is notified within two weeks of its receipt and he/she receives a very carefully crafted letter indicating precisely what the deficiency is as determined by the faculty. There are levels of acceptance as well – with honors (rare but occasional), as presented (most common), with minor revisions which are clearly specified (occasional), with major revisions (seldom), and rejected (rare, indeed). When a rejection does occur, one of the Foundation faculty is immediately assigned to the student with the expectation that the student will graduate the following year with careful faculty oversight. It nearly always is successful.

With respect to the academic degrees, the Foundation requires a thesis of 35,000 to 40,000 words for the master's and a dissertation requiring 45,000 to 60,000 words for the academic doctorates. Unlike the Project Consultant in the professional degree programs, the thesis and dissertation require an approved academic whose duties in the supervision of the exit project carries with it a stipend: $500.00 for a thesis and $1,000.00 for a dissertation. The Ordinarius (a traditional term for the dissertation supervisor) must be approved by the Foundation on the basis of a curriculum vitae and a scholarly reputation in the field of supervision.

Most Ordinarii are members of distinguished academic, research, or medical institutions and have the responsibility of bringing the student to a level of original contribution to the field of research such that the Ordinarius signs a document placing his/her reputation along side the merits of the finished product. This role is crucial in the overall evaluation process. When the student, therefore, comes for the oral defense before the Foundation's faculty, confidence is high on our part that the student will be successful owing to the sign-off of the Ordinarius. Again, as with professional degrees, there are gradations of completion and acceptance and, at the end of the day, many of these dissertations are published by the leading houses in the country. Again, as with the professional degree students, many times the academic degree students find themselves experiencing professional benefits by having selected an Ordinarius or thesis supervisor who is in a position of providing assistance in the advancement of their own careers.

We have no books, only the World Wide Web!

The academic degrees of the Foundation are library-based research. And, though the professional degrees are "praxis" oriented, access to a research library is always necessary for the completion of the project. So access to a research-level library is indispensable to all of our students. Yet, as has already been pointed out, the Foundation does not maintain a physical library.

That's not to say we are anti-bibliophiles! The question is not whether one is able to hold the book in one's hand but whether one has access to the contents of publications relevant to a serious piece of research. As studies have shown, and as has already been mentioned, a high percentage of utilization of the library, particularly by resident college students, is for something other than research – a quiet place to study, a convenient place to rendezvous with friends, or an easily accessible place to catch up on the newspaper and magazine reading.

We wish not to disparage the importance of the library for doctoral-level study. What we wish to point out is that access to research and scholarly materials need not be limited to a physical library, or, indeed, directly involve it at all. At this moment, the Foundation has over fifty doctoral students doing high-level original research in Eastern Europe, Latin America, and Southeast Asia, who do not immediately have access to a physical library but are busily, nonetheless, doing their research online. Why have the World Wide Web if it is not going to be utilized by those who can most benefit from it? The Foundation, at the time of the Orientation Session, provides each student with a forty-page directory of internet libraries, both full text and bibliographic. Since nearly 40% of our students are in some field of pastoral care and counseling and, thus, directly related to the health professions, we find that the utilization of the American Medical Association's full text online library, called Pub Med, is indispensable.

In every field of study at the Foundation – management, pastoral ministry, sacred music, mediation, Islamic Studies, Judaica, theology, philosophy, psychology, counseling, the creative arts, and media – we provide a roster of available internet libraries where students can do doctoral-level research either free or at very little cost. Early on in the history of the internet libraries, we purchased access to the leading internet library and passed along a modest fee to the students. After several years and with the radically exponential acceleration of new libraries coming online, it became clear that a roster of available internet library addresses would serve our students more effectively than subscribing to a single provider. The level of research being produced by Foundation students is testified to both by our international faculty evaluators as well as by the number of theses and dissertations being published annually by our graduating students.

In addition to having access to an internet research library second to no physical library (excepting the Library of Congress which itself is to be a full text internet library in just a few years), one must not forget Amazon.com and its cognates. Here any student anywhere in the world can purchase a desired text (even a used copy) at a very competitive price and have the book in hand in just a few days. This screening device necessarily built into the internet book-buying process, namely, buying and waiting, often serves the student's best interest in encouraging thoughtful consideration before a purchase is made, knowing, as I do, that the buying of a book is often the best substitute for actually reading it. I make this rather forlorn observation as I sit writing this book in my own library with walls and walls of books, some of which I have read!

Finally, and not to be ignored or forgotten, there is always Borders and Barnes & Noble as well as a plethora of independent new and used bookstores around the town, the country, and the world where one may visit, either online or in person, in search of just that relevant text. Often, it is easier to "Google" one's search for a special title than it is to visit various physical libraries in hopes of finding the right book. Try calling a university or public library and ask for a special title and see how helpful one finds the clerical or reference staff! Just Google the search and the book is usually found. We cannot let the absence of an accessible physical library disqualify an institution from offering doctoral-level degrees, not since the coming of the World Wide Web. The Foundation contains costs and elevates its student-performance expectations in consort with the utilization of internet library research which is available to everyone at all times and in all places.

We have no campus – we use the world's.

As with the library, so with the campus. We haven't one! That is to say, we don't have a physical library; rather, we send our students out into the World Wide Web's library resources which are almost limitless. Likewise, we do not maintain a campus owing to the fact that our students come to us for a one-day Orientation Session and return to us for a two-day Convocation and Graduation ceremony, staying in the Marriott Hotel and utilizing the Civic Center of South Bend for these grand occasions. Our campus is the world by which we mean at any given moment we have over 350 students studying at over 200 academic, research, study centers around the country and around the world. Our students are on university campuses, research institutes, learning venues of all kinds in the U.S. and around the world.

Our students do have a campus, but it's not ours. Rather, the hosting institutions where our students are taking a Unit of Study or earning graduate credits for a course being taken constitutes the campus at the moment. We do have a small and elegantly manicured city park adjacent to our facilities in The Tower Building on the courthouse square in downtown South Bend to which we refer affectionately as the Foundation's city campus! It is convenient, beautiful, and tax-payer supported and maintained. The issue for the Foundation has nothing to do with providing a lovely place to live and learn, study and research, for it is not at the Foundation that these things occur. We collaborate with student-clients in the development and maintenance of their personally created educational portfolio. The living and learning, studying and researching, occurs wherever and whenever they choose.

Another feature, just now being researched and studied by traditional institutions and learning venues, is the timelessness of the internet library research facilities. Gone are the days when one can only do research at the convenience of the library staff's working hours. As convenient as your nearest internet-accessible computer, any time of the day or night, anywhere in the world, just "go online" and commence your work. Sitting in one's pajamas at 2 a.m. with a warm cup of hot chocolate, plowing away on the dissertation when the juices are flowing and one is undisturbed by a shushing librarian or the buzz of a busy day that's the way more and more serious work is being done.

We judge the product -- Exiting with Class.

I collect horror stories of the misdeeds of academic institutions and their faculty. Though I don't think of myself as a morbid creature, I have over the past twenty-two years as President of the Foundation and some forty years in higher education, found it somewhat amusing and often quite informative, these stories of the good, the bad, and the ugly when it comes to student/faculty, student/administration relationships. One of several consistent points of difficulty found in my study, *UNFINISHED BUSINESS*, has to do with the personalization of relationships between faculty and students, especially doctoral students and their faculty advisor/supervisor. The radical differentiation between teaching and evaluating that has historically characterized the Oxford/Cambridge model of learning seems to me quite wise. For there, the student studies with a tutor but is examined by someone else other than the tutor. Tutors are for teaching; examinations are for evaluation by those not directly involved in the student/teacher relationship.

There have been countless stories of "personality conflicts" in which the students and faculty find themselves locked in a life-or-death relationship, a struggle which is too often fraught with pitfalls, it seems to me. What is needed and what 'the Foundation has evolved is a system whereby the student collects his/her Units of Study at venues of personal choice, followed by the selection of a Project Consultant (for professional degrees) or Ordinarius (for academic doctorates) of the student's choice, followed by an evaluation process under the oversight of the relevant faculty at the Foundation, allowing, at each juncture, for the stifling of "personal agendas" in the evaluation of student work.

Since the Foundation is non-creedal in its philosophy (we have virtually every branch of Christianity, Judaism, Islam and humanism represented in our faculty, our institutional relationships, and our student body), we have avoided quite nicely any disputes related to "faith and dogma" issues. Once, I remember, an Orthodox rabbi on our faculty chaired a doctoral defense of a Reformed rabbinic student to the success of the student and with the observation of the rabbinic faculty person in these words: "His defense was brilliant though I didn't agree with a thing he said in the two hour session!"

With the professional projects, we ask the Project Consultant to submit a multi-page evaluation form along with a narrative response to the overall process and the finished product. The Project Consultant does not, however, have any jurisdiction over the pass/fail options of the Foundation faculty. We want to see what the Project Consultant had to say about the process and the product, but the faculty reserves the exclusive right of final approval.

With the doctoral dissertation, the rules are slightly different in that the Foundation faculty requires that the Ordinarius sign a supporting statement relative to the dissertation prior to the defense. In the absence of this supporting statement of the Ordinarius, the student's defense cannot be held. Therefore, the student is under pressure to make sure that the selection of the Ordinarius is a personal fit as well as a scholarly one. Then, when the defense occurs, the faculty have high confidence and expectation of a successful defense, though the defense is certainly not *pro forma*. The faculty must agree in order for the student to receive the degree, but these faculty are judging the finished product separate and apart from any chance of personal issues being involved since the student's educational units have been taken elsewhere. The dissertation has been directed by an outside scholar in the field of which the faculty have already approved. The entire design of this process has been in the interest of protecting the student from "institutional agendas" and "faculty agendas" while assuring the student, faculty, and administration of the prospects of a quality piece of research.

We complete the agenda, from portfolio to graduation.

We have already mentioned the high percentage of uncompleted doctoral programs in theology which seem to unfortunately characterize the American landscape. The problems and solutions have been discussed in depth, based on data gathered from the leading institutions in the field, in my book mentioned earlier, *UNFINISHED BUSINESS.* The Foundation, from its inception, was determined to be of service to the ministry community and not a deterrent. The Foundation has been committed at all times to seeing to it that the professional practitioner seeking a terminal degree would, if merited, receive a terminal degree with no games, no hoops, no hidden agendas. We set out to establish a concept of the New Paradigm by creating the educational portfolio which would lead to a terminal degree in a cognate of ministry.

The portfolio lies at the heart of the New Paradigm, a plan which allows for the seasoned veteran as student-client to essentially design his/her own degree program by drawing from a plethora of educational venues available to him/her for the asking. From the accumulation of Units of Study at distinguished educational venues around the world, the student-client moves on to the writing of the terminal project – professional or academic. Finally, the professional degree project is submitted to the faculty in written form and the academic degree project is submitted in written form and orally defended. Once presented and defended, only the Convocation and Graduation stands between Foundation students and their terminal degrees.

Our Convocations and Graduations are grand occasions of celebration. And rightly so, too, given the years of service and the amount of work expended in the profession and in pursuit of the degree. Ministry professionals so seldom find an opportunity to celebrate their own accomplishments; rather, they spend most of their time encouraging others, celebrating others, making others feel good about their accomplishments in life -- births, marriages, anniversaries. The Convocation and Graduation of the Foundation are designed specifically to celebrate the student, the professional veteran who has spent his/her life making others feel good about their efforts and the achievements.

As we have little occasion to cluster our students together other than at the Orientation Sessions and at Graduation, we make the most of the event. Our Convocations bring together our students from all over the world, from every type of ministry and service job, from every walk of life, from every religious and humanistic tradition. Our Convocations bring international figures from various traditions -- Christian, Jewish, Muslim -- and the evening address is followed by a grand social. The Graduation ceremony is held in the city Civic Center's Recital Hall, once again utilizing a tax-payer funded institution for public celebrations. Why do we have to build more and more private meeting halls when we pay for the building of beautiful public facilities? Is it pride? Is it a sense of ownership by an institution rather than a corporate sense of community ownership?

CONCLUDING REMARKS

From the outset we have been suggesting that the P.R.I.M.E. factor constitutes a New Paradigm of collaborative education. Indeed, we have ventured to call it a "radical philosophy" owing to its outside-the-box approach to institutional cooperation in the sharing of resources. We have not suggested that this is the first time in higher education that institutions have been called upon to collaborate. Collaboration has been occurring in higher education for centuries. One need only take a look at the history of the relationship between Cambridge and Oxford to see the special nature of these ancient clubs' working together.

What we have done, however, is to elevate institutional collaboration to a formula of procedure in the development of a

New Paradigm of higher education geared specifically to the veteran students as seasoned practitioners. We have rather ruthlessly savaged the traditionalist institutions for having presumed in the dealing with professional practitioners returning for terminal degrees in the same knee-jerk reaction as with undergraduate students. The putting in place of a completely stand-alone degree program, take-it-or-leave-it thank-you-very-much mentality simply will not work for these professional people. A new posture of relationship between these professionals and the hosting institution is called for, and we have both proposed a model and demonstrated in our forty-two years that it works well for both students and institutions.

The Foundation has never presumed that our way is the only way. Indeed, we occasionally have inquiring students who come, wishing to have all of the questions answered and all of the problems solved by simply handing them a list of courses to take in order to get the degree. These students we send on to the better traditionalist institutions and, quite often, they successfully complete their studies. No, the Foundation is only really interested in those professional practitioners who are sufficiently well placed as to not even consider leaving their employment to pursue a terminal degree but, nevertheless, are most eager to secure the doctorate as the final cap on their professional training. These are the students who are interesting to the Foundation and the constituency for whom we desire to be of service.

As an alternative to the physical campus, book-filled library, retail bookstore, tenured faculty, and sports program and arena the envy of all, the Foundation rather prefers to embrace the internet for its campus, its library, its bookstore, its faculty, and, well, CNN sports broadcasts serve our limited sports interest. We are serving the professional veteran involved in the practice of his/her profession such that "moving onto campus" or "going to class" are simply not options either available or attractive.

Cost containment is, of course, another great benefit of the Foundation's New Paradigm of collaborative education, for we

111

ask the student to pay for the administrative cost of managing the educational portfolio and keeping our collaborative inter-institutional relationships rather than libraries, faculties, bookstores, and sports programs. And, by doing so, our Ph.D. costs less than $10,000.00, opposed to $100,000.00 at top U.S. universities! We also throw into the bargain an opportunity for our student-clients to study at Oxford, Rome, Vienna, Zurich, Louvain, and a plethora of other national and institutionally distinguished research institutes.

Partnering resources in ministry education, the New Paradigm called "The P.R.I.M.E. Factor," is here to stay. The Foundation has elevated collegial consultation to an institutional philosophy, and has demonstrated in more than four decades and over 1,500 professional graduates that the New Paradigm works well for those for whom it has been created. Not just the two dozen bishops we have produced, the three college presidents, the dozen or so academic deans, the scores of seminary and university faculty, the senior administrative officers at national denominational headquarters, and chief personnel in the dioceses and archdioceses of America, the distinguished Imams and outstanding rabbinic representatives, but the hundreds of others – pastors, counselors, administrators, health care workers, chaplains, musicians, mediators, and freelance writers also who have come through our program all bespeak of an educational venture which is successfully addressing an educational need in the helping professions, a need not met by the "residential" program requiring years of on-campus, professionally disengaged study.

There is room for both models, the Old Paradigm and the New Paradigm, and there is an ongoing need for both as well. The New Paradigm will, however, find itself being sought after by the self-starting, personally self-disciplined professional veteran with a vision of the future not present in the Old Paradigm cookie-cutter student and institution. The New Paradigm student will use the PRIME FACTOR to further professional skills and development within the context of a continuing practice of ministry without interruption. The PRIME FACTOR will serve this particular type of professional rather well by providing a wide latitude of educational venues, a freedom to develop a personal educational agenda, and the capacity to afford to venture into new territory of ministry practice, all the while maintaining employment and containing cost.

Those interested in learning more about the Graduate Theological Foundation are invited to visit our website at www.gtfeducation.org and/or call for a complete information packet, without obligation, to 1-800-423-5983 in the U.S. and Canada or to 1-574-287-3642 elsewhere in the world. Of course, anyone may email the Foundation anytime at gtfed@sbcglobal.net.

ABOUT THE AUTHOR

John H. Morgan, Ph.D. (Hartford Seminary Foundation), D.Sc. (College of Applied Sciences/London), Psy.D. (Foundation House/Oxford), is the Karl Mannheim Professor of the History and Philosophy of Social Sciences at the Graduate Theological Foundation in Indiana where he has also been President since 1982. Since 1998, he has been teaching in the University of Oxford Summer Programme in Theology where he was appointed to the Board of Studies in 1995. He has held postdoctoral appointments at Harvard, Yale, and Princeton and has been a National Science Foundation Science Faculty Fellow at the University of Notre Dame. He has also held three postdoctoral appointments to the University of Chicago. The author of over thirty books and scores of scholarly articles, his latest books include *NATURALLY GOOD: Human Behavior and Moral Development (from Charles Darwin to E. O. Wilson), 2005; UNFINISHED BUSINESS: The Terminal All-But-Dissertation Phenomenon in American Higher Education (A National Study of Doctoral Programs in Theology), 2004;* and *BEING HUMAN: Perspectives in Meaning and Interpretation (Essays in Religion, Culture, and Personality), 2003.*